AESTHETICA BOTANICA

A Life with Plants

GINGKO PRESS

AESTHETICA BOTANICA

A Life with Plants

First Published in the USA by
Gingko Press by arrangement with
Sandu Publishing Co., Ltd.

Gingko Press, Inc.
1321 Fifth Street
Berkeley, CA 94710 USA
Tel: (510) 898 1195
Fax: (510) 898 1196
Email: books@gingkopress.com
www.gingkopress.com

ISBN 978-1-58423-686-3

Sponsored by Design 360°–
Concept & Design Magazine

Edited and produced by
Sandu Publishing Co., Ltd.

Book design, concepts & art direction by
Sandu Publishing Co., Ltd.
Chief Editor: Wang Shaoqiang
Design Director: Niu Huizhen
Copy Editor: Jason Buchholz

Illustration on front cover by Compañía Botánica.
Illustration on back cover by Olga Prinku,
Angelo Dal Bó, Loose Leaf, Karen Suehiro, India Hobson.
Index illustrations by Chow Pakwah.

info@sandupublishing.com
www.sandupublishing.com

Printed and bound in China

Contents

Miniature

Preface

By Josh Rosen

The connection between plants and people is a deep and enduring one. A powerful evolutionary cue links the human mind and body to the botanical world. It may be a subconscious recognition of the plants' role in sustaining all aspects of life—creating everything from the oxygen we breathe, the food we eat, to even the clothes we wear. Without plants human life on our planet would not exist. Beyond the plants' responsibility for our very lives, they are also sources of inspiration and relaxation for humans bombarded by the stresses of modern life and its symptomatic separation from nature. By rediscovering this connection, the designers, artists, and florists featured in this book have found unique ways to bring the botanical world back into our lives.

Whether in a home, studio, or workshop, plants can define a space. Our living spaces often suffer from a lack of connection with nature. The effect on inhabitants can be dramatic, from both mental and physical perspectives. Countless studies have shown the benefits of incorporating plant life into our living and work spaces. Mental acuity, lower stress levels, and an increased sense of well-being are all reported. In addition, plants have been shown to filter toxins from the air and provide valuable oxygen. Something within the human brain turns on when it witnesses green leaves engaging in photosynthesis and the more we can bring this special interaction into our environments, the happier and more productive we are.

In addition to the scientific benefits provided by plant life, there is an intangible benefit provided by the process of caring for these living creatures. The simple acts of observing a plant's health and providing the watering and the other care it requires have innumerable benefits. As humans we intrinsically benefit from this connection with a life form and process beyond ourselves. The "monkey mind" of our scattered thoughts can be focused and falls away as we engage in these simple nourishing activities. Once we recognize the vital role of plant life in human well-being we have the opportunity to expand the consideration to aesthetics. The three parts of *Aesthetica Botanica* focus on different aspects: Floral, Lush Leaf, and Miniature. Each of these parts highlights a different area of botanical aesthetic inspiration. This includes the powerful colors of floral displays, the full green depth of leaves, and the unusual miniature aspects of plants from mosses to succulents. The botanical world offers a range of scales, colors, and forms to intrigue the aesthetic senses and the designers featured have each followed different paths to create their art.

Plants have inspired art and aesthetics throughout history. Ancient cave drawings depict the plants and animals that supported life from its origins. From this time on humans have looked to the botanical world for inspiration. The color and form of flowers, the patterns of foliage, and the golden mean ratio found in so many species' growth patterns have even connected the human mind with the underlying mathematical principals that govern life.

In the modern world of social media, plants and images of how they are integrated into our living spaces are among the most popular. Bloggers have recognized the value and appeal these spaces and inspiration provide. This popularity taps into a desire to reclaim our botanical heritage and re-connect with nature. When a thoughtful aesthetic is also introduced to botanical displays, the enthusiasm is remarkable.

It is unclear where botanical design will go next. Artists are newly inspired to design with plants every day and trends are hard to predict. What one can safely assume, however, is that humans will continue to be moved by botanical art and seek to elevate it and bring it into their lives. This art can take many forms but will undoubtedly return to its "root" in the natural world while also highlighting the designer's hand, which is inspired by the nourishing role of the botanical world in all our lives.

To observe its color, to sense its touch, to embrace its fragrance, and to be friends with nature. This book is dedicated to all those who care for plants, love connecting with nature, and enjoy life.

Lush Leaf

"Living with plants is a task that you have to be fully dedicated to. These are living things here that we're talking about."

— Hilton Carter

Nature Nursery

A Place of Leisure

•

"I'd describe my aesthetic as simple, minimal, and green. As the years have gone by, I've begun to appreciate the notion that less is more."

•

Mégan Twilegar

Out of a deep love for plants and the need to pursue something she loves, Mégan Twilegar founded Pistils Nursery in 2001. As more and more people are intrigued by the idea of the urban jungle, it has become a fabulous place that is truly worthy of the name "nursery," a place that enables visitors to envision a simple, greener life for themselves—whether it be an outdoor garden or an interior rewilding of one's home.

- **Occupation:** *Shop owner, designer*
- **Location:** *Portland, Oregon, USA*

Situated in Portland, Oregon, a city that has been at the forefront of the urban chicken husbandry movement since the early 2000s, Pistils Nursery was initially an urban farm store. It is now a green paradise where Mégan Twilegar pursues her love for indoor and outdoor plants. A newly added solarium at Pistils allows sunlight to shine down on the plants as chickens roam around. Mégan's original intention for the solarium was to design a space that would always be bright with natural light, creating an optimal environment to host plants from far afield. "We wanted to create a tropical oasis in the heart of the city that

folks would never want to leave. Therefore, the idea of augmenting our indoor space by creating a solarium with lots of light made total sense. It has done wonders for Pistils. When we look back on it, we can't imagine how we ever lived without it," says Mégan.

Pistils also contains many decorative objects; each has its own unique past. The bricks in the solarium came from a chimney that was removed from an old house under renovation, and the sink used for soaking plants every day was found at a salvage yard. The central table, with its incredible colors and pattern, was made from a piece of salvaged Asian hardwood.

◀ Shrubs, perennials, and trees outside Pistils.

▲ Mounted epiphytic Hoyas and Dischidias, a large variegated Euphorbia, and assorted succulents and cacti.

The staff at Pistils are fascinated with the challenge of finding new places to source tropical plants, so far from their native habitats. "Every plant is different so caring for houseplants requires a lot of patience and practice. Over time, you'll learn the needs of your houseplants, and how to create a care regimen according to the environmental conditions of your home, like light, temperature, and humidity," Mégan says.

Over the years, Mégan has come to understand that recalibrating the business from time to time is paramount to being successful. She and her staff have witnessed many trends come and go. They have embraced them and passed the torches as well. They are striving to become one of the most robust, eclectic, and inspiring plant shops in Portland. Looking into the future, Mégan says, "We're happy with the trajectory that Pistils has taken over the last few years. We started with just our brick-and-mortar. Over the years, we've added a landscape design division, interior plantscaping division, an online shop, workshops, and even created our product line. We are content with working on further development and the refinement of our current business, for example, by adding new workshops and creating new products for our visitors. We may even consider opening a second location shortly."

◄ This sink, which is used for daily watering, was found at a salvage yard by Mégan.

▲ Staghorn ferns on the wall, assorted Tillandsia and bromeliads in the sink, and an Anthurium veitchii in a pot.

▼ Haley caring for a mounted staghorn fern.

▲ A large staghorn fern, surrounded by tropical houseplants, enjoying a sunbath in the solarium.

➤ Cody holding a moosehorn fern.

1. We know that Pistils Nursery has a collection of flora and fauna. Why did you choose to raise chickens?

Keeping chickens is very easy compared to keeping other farm animals, especially in the city on small urban lots. We used to sell chickens as part of our store offerings, and have always had our own flock of chickens in order to show our visitors how they might keep chickens in their own yards. As the years have gone by and more nurseries have begun selling chicks and pullets, we no longer offer this as part of the business. But our own flock continues to live on-site as a way to honor the history of the shop, because we love them! They can definitely do damage in the garden if allowed access. They can ravage gardens—especially love tender vegetables and ferns—if let free-range. It's best to keep them confined in a generously sized run and let them out for small periods of supervised time.

2. Do you think Portland is a good place for plants?

Portland's mild, maritime climate is a very desirable climate in which to garden outdoors. Our gardening season is very long, because we're close to the Pacific. As a result, many thousands of plants species that aren't native to Oregon can be grown here and live happily outdoors. This is heaven to those who are plant-obsessed and wish to try to grow things that are from far afield. Unfortunately, the climate here in Portland isn't as ideal for some of our indoor plants. The days get quite short during winter, and most days are cloudy or even rainy, which means that light is scarce. Desert plants like cacti and succulents have a hard time getting enough light to thrive here during the winter in your typical Portland home. We only recommend these plants to folks who have especially sunny spots, or are able to supplement with grow lights or full-spectrum bulbs. Most tropical plants are okay here during the winter, though they don't necessarily produce a ton of growth this time of year. Any indoor plant is going to require less water during the winter than during the spring and summertime.

As our own interests have changed and new plants call out to us, we've done our best to stay present with the times and, at best, to become trendsetters.

◄ A vintage cabinet adds a unique charm.
▲ Ariana, watering the plants in the solarium.
▼ Plants thrive in all corners of Pistils' solarium.

3. We noticed that you use the hashtag #InteriorRewilding online. Please tell us more about it.

One of our reasons for starting Pistils was to cultivate and connect a community of plant lovers. The increasing popularity of social media platforms like Instagram has allowed us to expand our local community and connect with folks living all over the world, which is very inspiring to us.

In addition to sharing images of our own greenery, we love seeing what other people are able to create with plants in their homes and gardens. One way we've encouraged people to connect with us is by using hashtags, so that we can find and spotlight their photos. We've used a number of hashtags over the years.

4. What impresses you most about living with plants?

I feel it's akin to a living journal. Each plant I acquire takes me back to that time in my life—where I was living, what I was doing. Oftentimes plants in my garden remind me of people who have been a part of my life, still and sometimes no longer. When I walk around my outdoor garden I see lots of people from whom I have learned and who shared the passion of loving plants and nature as I do.

5. What are your top tips of caring plants?

- Identify your plant.
- Know your space.
- Choose the right pot.
- Carefully re-pot and pot up.
- Remember: less is more.
- Use the "finger test."
- Water slowly and thoroughly.

▲ Using an Aspenium (an "austral gem") fern to make a kokedama.
▼ Epiphytic tropical plants and jungle cacti mounted on cork.
▶ The entrance of the solarium.

▲ ➤ Pistils Nursery displays plants in different forms, such as these terrariums of succulents, airplants in baskets, wall-mounted staghorns, and plantlets arranged on a shelf.

"I appreciate not just the bloom of a plant, but so much more—for example the underside of a leaf, the growth habit, the peeling or flaking bark. All these things should be embraced."

Pinkish Greenery
The Painted Plants

•

"The most satisfying aspect of living with plants is seeing their growth and progress when you care for them properly."

•

Chelsae Anne and Evan Sahlman

Chelsae and Evan turned their 1920's apartment into a plant-filled bohemian oasis which is described as "modern meets the eccentric romantic." Chelsae and Evan's art backgrounds contribute to their pursuit of their dreams, helping them understand beauty and how to draw people's attention to it. With personalized touches and a lot of planning, they transformed their place into a cozy pinkish space with easy additions.

• **Occupation:** *Photographer, artist*
• **Location:** *West Palm Beach, Florida, USA*

Chelsae Anne is a full-time freelance photographer specializing in lifestyle, editorial, and portrait photography; Evan Sahlman is the owner and art director of Sahlman Studio and is adept in pottery, ceramics, and sculpture. They met each other in the first year of college and started dating two years later. They learned about each other's lives, goals, and dreams and admire each other's talents and interests. Their backgrounds in visual art enables them to apply professional principles to their work and life.

This couple lives in West Palm Beach—a famous tourist attraction where elites gather and a great place to call home. Their home is situated in an old building that was built in the 1920s. In the beginning, they considered it to be a short-term rental where they would live until they could find somewhere more beautiful. To make the place feel less like a rented room, Chelsae and Evan started to make small updates to maximize their living space and reflect their tastes.

◀ The living room is a cozy space with tropical plants and the pink tones of Evan's painting.
▲ Evan, standing in the living room.
▼ A corner where Chelsae and Evan spend time reading.

West Palm Beach is amazingly rich in plants, both in variety and quantity. Being surrounded by a diverse botanical environment, they are greatly inspired by the ways plants give life and colors to spaces. Thus, they gradually transformed the place into a calm and chic oasis, decorating it with vintage furniture sourced from thrift markets and plants of all sorts, from windowsill succulents to larger floor plants and leafy strands collected from nurseries. Their home has become a place full of life, joy, and love.

Besides their 1920s home, Chelsae and Evan also own a gallery and a warehouse studio. As photographer and artist, this couple needed a public space where people could come and see their creative work. They hold exhibitions from time to time, which bring pressure but also a sense of achievement. Chelsae says, "When Evan exhibits in a gallery, there is always the pressure of time and quality. For the last few shows he held, he was able to produce new projects in a very short time by working fourteen hours a day regularly. He doesn't always need to push limits in this way, but he takes the quality of his work seriously."

Chelsae and Evan have traveled extensively throughout North America, Europe, and New Zealand. Their goal is to continue documenting the world around them and exploring the unknown. They are always ready to move on to the next adventure.

◀ ▲ The apartment is filled with vintage ornaments, decorations collected from trips, and stylish photographs.

▲ ▶ Bohemia plays an important role in the apartment, infusing the bedroom with coziness. Plants of all sizes bring greenery to the space. Chelsae's cats nestle in the soft blankets.

1. You keep various kinds of plants in your home. Why do you choose plants as your major decorative elements?

We use a lot of plants to design our space because of the beautiful shapes and colors that only they can offer. They offer an ever-changing sculptural aspect to a space. As they grow and expand, they also change the way our space looks and feels.

2. How would you describe your aesthetic?

I would say our aesthetic is based on a deep background of art appreciation. When we find furniture or plants that we want to integrate into our space, we are careful to make sure that every individual piece could stand alone and be visually pleasing itself.

3. Your place is both vintage and lively. Would you tell us more about your process of reconstruction?

After we'd been here for a year we started to do little things, like painting the walls and cabinets in our kitchen. Then we saw that there was real potential to create a home here that we could be proud of. We worked on bigger projects, like our shelf wall, and Evan built our four-poster platform bed specifically for our space.

It was starting to come together piece-by-piece with mid-century chairs and tall birds of paradise. This was the fun stage, when we would go to thrift stores and nurseries and look for the perfect pieces to add. We still go looking for treasures when we feel we want to change something out.

4. There are many ornaments in your house collected from antique markets. Is there a particular piece that means a lot to you?

Some of the pieces we greatly cherish are our mid-century lounge chairs, designed by Kofod Larsen. We have rearranged and updated our home multiple times but they have stayed with us the entire duration.

"

As artists, we find it important to be surrounded by beautiful and inspiring spaces and we strive to always improve upon what we already have.

"

◀ Evan's painted cacti on the wall.

▲ ▼ The living room is a project this couple staged and styled and turned into a pop-up art gallery for Evan's art and a few of Chelsae's photographs.

We are also very attached to our chandeliers, especially the solid brass floral chandelier hanging above our bed. It has definitely added a sense of luxury to a fairly down-to-earth home.

5. Pink is the main tone in your works. Why do you choose to work in this color?

Pink is a color that can be misleading sometimes. But as we refine our palettes, we have fallen in love with the blush skin tone that is more neutral than what you may picture in your mind. For Evan, the fondness was sparked by a trip to a Miami art fair years ago.

Out of hundreds of works of art, only a few stood out—abstract pieces that had large bold strokes of pink running through the centers. This stuck with him and last year he started to apply a similar tone while working on a series of cacti paintings.

6. You have traveled extensively. Is there a particular place that you like most, so far?

We have both traveled our whole lives, starting at a young age with our families. I and my family lived in Nigeria for three years and Evan in Argentina for four years. Since then we have experienced more than twenty other countries and we loved every place we've been for different reasons. A few places that stand out above and beyond the rest are the deserts of Morocco and the beauty of New Zealand. A stark contrast in landscape and culture yet they fall into the most memorable experiences.

▲ ▶ Evan painting.
▼ Plant care in the gallery.

▲ ▼ ➤ Evan's paintings capture the plants' verve and showcase their vigor and vitality.
He holds exhibitions from time to time.

"When you're studying art you have to learn about the basics, from the Renaissance up to now. It gives you an understanding about what is beautiful and why people are drawn to it."

Dance in Green

A Maker of Things

•

"Greenery in the home has so many positive attributes. The more you have, the better you feel."

•

Hilton Carter

Hilton Carter turned a converted cotton mill into his greenhouse. Entering it is like stepping into an indoor forest made of living artwork with a mysterious glamour. The whole interior reconstruction is a true reflection of his personality, his style, and most of all, his dream.

- **Occupation:** *Interior designer, artist, and filmmaker*
- **Location:** *Baltimore, Maryland, USA*

After graduating from the Maryland Institute College of Art, Hilton Carter headed to Los Angeles to further his study and received his MFA in Film there. He lived in LA for many years and then moved to New Orleans for a small stint.

While in New Orleans, he was offered a job at an advertising agency in his hometown of Baltimore, MD. Loving the city of Baltimore as he does and knowing that his family was still there made it an easy choice to move back.

Hilton now lives with his girlfriend, Fiona, in an 1870s historic cotton mill, located in the heart of Baltimore and right next to the Jones Falls. The windows are tall and large enough to let in plenty of sunlight for his houseplants. When looking out through them, he sees trees, the river, and other natural scenery. Talking about his original intention of settling here, Hilton says, "I was looking for a loft-style apartment and some friends mentioned that this one had just opened up and that I should go and check it out. I did and clearly loved it!"

◀ Hilton's living room is stylishly decorated.
▲ A bedroom nook where Fiona spends time reading.

An interior designer himself, Hilton gave more thought to the décor and did a lot of reconstruction on his house. The aesthetic of his place is described as "a mash-up of urban modern, industrial, and bohemian." There are a lot of vintage pieces sourced from flea markets and thrift stores, adding vitality to the house. One wall in the home is a living plant wall filled with lush tubes. In his bedroom, a creative plant canopy hangs over the bed. The canopy was initially a large philodendron from Hilton's mother, but she ran out of room for it. Hilton then sketched out an idea for hanging it on the wall because at that time Fiona was really into making macramé hangers. He and Fiona turned it into a hammock-like project which is now one of the highlights in his house.

Hilton always dreamed of connecting with plants in a natural way—like living in a greenhouse, for instance.

He started his collection with a single golden pothos and a few succulents and then proceeded onto larger purchases like a fiddle leaf fig and staghorn ferns. As time went by, he gradually acquired a vast collection of plants and turned his place into an indoor jungle. Hilton believes that a hint of natural green can elevate a minimalist décor scheme, extend the lush aesthetic of a bohemian space, and revitalize a gloomy interior. His mission is to create an interior green space that looks welcoming and inspiring—a place that never gets boring. To do this, he focuses on further reconstruction, cleans the air, and makes it feel more like home to him.

Hilton is also a freelance artist and filmmaker. He has created his own brand—Things by HC, a unique universe for his products, prints and all manner of other "things."

◄ Hilton's dog, Charlie, sitting in the nook.

▼ A corner of the bedroom.

➤ Green is the main feature in Hilton's apartment.

1. There's a living wall in your home where all the plants are growing from tubes. Why did you choose such a unique type of container?

Our living wall is made of vessels that I call "cradles." They are a product I designed and now sell via my website and in local stores in Baltimore. I decided on this type of style because unlike other living walls, this one is a propagation wall, so the cuttings placed on the wall can produce roots and then be potted. This allows you to not only have a wall full of greenery, but it is also a gift that keeps on giving.

2. Have you ever counted how many plants you own now? How do you manage to take care of them?

The last time I counted the number of plants we have it was a little more than one hundred and eighty. In order to take care of all of them, one, I set a reminder in my calendar each week to water them, and two, I make sure to place plants that need the same sort of light and attention together. This makes it easier to remember how much to water them and when. You just have to take them as a priority.

3. Where do you get inspiration, generally?

I guess most of it comes when I find myself needing to fix a problem. For example, I wanted a living wall in our home but couldn't afford the traditional version. So at the time I had a spice rack that I was using to propagate cuttings, and I said, "Why not just have a wall full of these racks?" That eventually sparked the idea for the cradle.

4. We noticed that you've done some reconstructions in your place, like painting the walls. Could you tell us more about it?

I painted two of the walls in the dining room area. They are basically painted to look worn and aged with a bit of a Jackson Pollock touch. There's just something about dripping paint and a good patina that I'm addicted to.

> " *Living with plants is a task that you have to be fully dedicated to. These are living things here that we're talking about.* "

◄ Hilton's cat, Isabella, hiding amongst the plants.
▲ Greenery in the hallway.

5. Your place has been described as "a mash-up of urban modern, industrial, and bohemian," which is equipped with a great amount of creative furniture. Where did you source the furniture? Is there a particular piece that means a lot to you?

We have collected furniture from all over the place, whether it's from a big store, flea market or handed down. We just really want pieces in our place that carry a story. My favorite piece is the mini Harley-Davidson that was handed down to me from my father. It was one of the things he saved up his money as a kid to purchase and over thirty years later it was given to me. It means a lot.

6. You're a painter and filmmaker, and now a botanical designer. How do you balance your roles in different fields?

I find a way to balance all of my creative outlets by utilizing all of my waking hours and by keeping a daily planner. If it's on the schedule it gets done, even if that means waking up at 4:30 a.m. to start my day and ending it at 1 a.m.. But this is only when necessary. I tend to wake up at 5:30 each morning and I'm in bed by midnight.

7. Would you share with us your philosophy on living with plants? Do you have any suggestions for beginners?

Living with plants is a task that you have to be fully dedicated to. These are living things here that we're talking about.

They'll need your full attention at least twice a week. And if you do your homework and know your plants well, they will thrive and continue to give you good air and comforting feelings, and add beauty to your home.

▲ A collection of plants and cacti.
▼ Hilton caring for his plants.
➤ The window where Hilton tries to place all of the cacti and succulents together so that he remembers to water them regularly.

▲ Detailed capture of a Monstera and a heart-shaped pothos.
➤ Hilton's plant tubes thrive on the cradle wall.

"The best part for me about living with plants is watching them grow and thrive. When they start to take on their own strange and unique look, that's when it gets fun."

Ivan Martinez and Christan Summers

Hit the Road

Mobile Greenhouse

•

"One of our mottos is 'Plants Are Alive.' We should not treat them as inanimate objects."

•

Ivan Martinez and Christan Summers

Ivan Martinez and Christan Summers, founders of Tula Plants and Design and the Tulita truck, are enamored with the plant world for its endless design possibilities. Unlike most traditional retail shops, they infuse Tula and Tulita with creativity. Ivan and Christan aim to improve the lifestyles of city dwellers by getting them closer to plants.

• **Occupation:** *Modern horticulturists, designers, and plant enthusiasts*
• **Location:** *Brooklyn, New York, USA*

From early ages, Ivan Martinez and Christan Summers were taught the value of caring for nature and the significance of integrating it into daily life. They both grew up surrounded by plants, and their love for nature and their similar educational backgrounds, in advertising, ultimately drew them together.

In New York, a city with little greenery, keeping indoor plants is a way for people to connect with nature. Tired of her full-time advertising gig, Christan was eager for such a connection. She started to learn horticulture on her own and found in Ivan someone who agreed that education and creativity should be valued in the plant world. To achieve their goals, they collaborated and planned, and eventually came up with a plant shop conception—the birth of Tula.

Tula is a beautiful greenhouse with various plants, open to the public. Ivan says, "Indoor plants are a way for city dwellers to find a little peace at the end of their busy days. It feels calm to be surrounded by plants. Caring for plants is a great way to forget about the stress from work or personal lives as you're thinking about the health of another living being. I like to say that plants are like pets, but greener." Tula also includes a mobile plant car, called the Tulita truck, which is painted a dark green color. The truck came to Christan's mind on one of her regular morning runs. Because of the high housing costs in Brooklyn, Christan believed that a mobile storefront would be a practical solution to reach more people and bring plants on the road. It is an innovative take on the traditional retail industry, and now markets its living products throughout Brooklyn and Manhattan.

◄ Entrance to Tula's Summer pop-up.

▲ Christan playing with a plant.

▼ Ivan is working to provide plants with more suitable living circumstances.

Ivan and Christan have always strived to steer Tula's business in a local and sustainable direction. Ivan works on Tula's branding, including the logo, aesthetic, visuals, and creative direction, while Christan concentrates on developing business plans and financial projections. When they realized that there was room in the market for them to create their own products, they began to collaborate with like-minded brands and local makers to offer some unique products. In 2017, they introduced apparel and accessories, limited editions of planter collections made in collaboration with local ceramicists, and t-shirts made from 100% recycled cotton in Los Angeles. "Our passion for plants has grown since we launched the business, and there is more to learn and inspire us!" says the couple.

In early 2018, Ivan and Christan were excited to announce the impending opening of their first retail storefront in Greenpoint, Brooklyn. "We're also working on Tula's first line of branded planters, which will be made in the US and designed in-house. In the next five years, we have plans to expand within the US and beyond. We have our eyes set on Southeast Asia! We also look forward to innovating the process of our production and growing our own plants. With lots of exciting things to come, we hope that we can update you with all of these dreams we have!" say Ivan and Christan with excitement.

◀ ▲ Lush green is the main characteristic in Tula's interior, along with clay pottery.

1. We understand that Tula was a greenhouse café at first. Why did you choose to turn it to a plant store?

The greenhouse café was the very first idea that propelled us down the road of creating Tula. Like all ideas, it evolved and took various forms and shapes along the way. This is an important process to ideation—you have to probe and poke holes into your first idea. Imagine yourself from start to finish and ask yourself simple questions: Who are the customers? What is the daily routine? Are you passionate about the product and service you'll be providing? We posed these same questions which helped us realize that our passion lies in plants and the innovation of objects and experiences to help people integrate the natural world into their lives. Which, who knows, may take us back to the greenhouse café one day!

2. You pay a lot of attention to your customers' demands and spend time teaching people about plant care. Why?

This is a great question and a really important aspect of the Tula brand. Prior to launching the company, we conducted a lot of market research and noticed that plant shops were not spending much time learning about their customers' environments and lifestyles. So we choose to spend a lot of time with each customer. We like to learn about their home so we can match them with the right plant. It's like a dating app and we are the matchmakers. We want them to feel as if they have all the information they need to keep their plant alive and growing for the long term.

3. You also cooperate with various designers in pottery and interior décor. Is design part of the Tula brand?

Yes, design is at the heart of Tula. Our goal is to offer objects and experiences that thoughtfully integrate the natural world into our customers' daily lives. With design, it is increasingly important to think about how and what an object is made from and what the production could or could not be affecting

66

Our goal is to make every customer feel confident when they leave with a new plant.

99

▲ The dark green mobile greenhouse—Tulita.

◀ ▼ The Tulita truck attracts people to walk in and explore.

in the process. It is no secret the world faces serious environmental issues so as Tula continues to grow and we create more objects, we strive to innovate production in order to keep our company's footprint the smallest it can be.

4. Here's one question for Christan: On Tula's web profile, it mentions that you lived in Paris and Bangkok once, and you even swam with sharks. Would you please tell us more about those experiences?

These are great memories. Swimming with sharks happened in my childhood. My mom is a photographer and took us with her on expeditions to the Galapagos Islands. One day we joined her snorkeling and we were soon swimming with nurse sharks and hammerheads. I was very scared at first, but then slowly calmed down when I realized they were not looking at me as food!

I moved to Bangkok in 2008 and lived there for roughly five months to source a factory to manufacture a jewelry line I co-designed with another artist. We successfully sourced a women-led factory and made a twenty-six-piece gold and silver jewelry collection. Then I moved to Paris with a plan to distribute the collection. I ended up staying and lived in Paris for four years. While I was there I started my first business, which was an online shop for unique jewelry and accessories. They were beautiful experiences that taught me so much.

5. Can you tell us more about your motto, "Plants are Alive"?

Yes, plants are absolutely, one hundred percent alive. They are living, breathing beings that react to light and vibrations. They require nutrients to survive—food, water and oxygen, just like us! Plants can see light and sense gravity. They "talk" to each other and thrive in social settings. When you begin to think of plants this way it really changes your whole perception of nature.

▲ Earthen pots are an important feature at Tula.
▼ Plants hang on the wire rack for selling.
▶ The Tulita truck has become a scenic spot on New York's streets.

▲ ▼ ➤ Leafy plants are the main feature in Tula.

"Plant facts are mind blowing—how fascinating plant life is and it excites us that there is still so much to learn."

Nurture in Nature

Loose Leaf

•

"Working with nature is in our bones; we just happened to come across a career that combined our skills and allowed us to work creatively with nature."

•

Wona Bae and Charlie Lawler

Loose Leaf, located in Collingwood, Melbourne, Australia, is a design studio by artists Wona Bae and Charlie Lawler. Their focus is concept-based art installations that use natural materials. Not only do they create unique botanical installations, but they collaborate with some well-established brands.

- **Occupation:** *Botanical artists, authors*
- **Location:** *Melbourne, Australia*

Wona Bae and Charlie Lawler share an innate desire to create a meaningful connection with nature through their designs. Wona has a Master of Floristry and Charlie, a Master of Design; the pair met in Germany while Wona was studying and it wasn't long before they began collaborating on small projects. From there they decided to move to Australia, and after several years working in their respective industries they created Loose Leaf—a concept-based art studio that combines their complementary skills. They describe Loose Leaf as a defining project, "a culmination of a long-awaited collaboration between us."

What started as a shared creative outlet for both Wona and Charlie soon evolved into something much more. Loose Leaf studio became home, where the pair experimented with new ideas and created large-scale botanical designs. In 2014 they opened a multifaceted concept space adjoining their studio, comprising a

retail store, a workshop for teaching classes, and a gallery. These five years saw Loose Leaf develop into a community hub for sharing local and international botanical creations, products, and knowledge.

Wona and Charlie's philosophy centers around creating with and reconnecting with nature—a constant source of inspiration for the artists. Loose Leaf studio is driven by the pair's keen interest to observe, study and explore natural materials; their installations may be made up of hundreds of dried flowers that have changed their appearance over time, or thousands of sticks weaved individually to make a stunning sculpture. Wona and Charlie's body of work highlights the interaction between natural systems and the built environment, and their use of natural materials reflects nature's beauty in all its phases and forms, even beyond its "best moment."

◀ ▲ ▼ Loose Leaf, Wona and Charlie's Collingwood studio.

Loose Leaf's installations encourage an interaction and participation, inviting the viewer to experience their artworks with a playful energy which is both thought-provoking and therapeutic. Wona and Charlie's ephemeral sculptures are a response to the surrounding environment and reflect the fragility of the natural world; they also give people an identifiable connection to the natural environment which can positively impact mental health and wellbeing.

Loose Leaf's more recent projects have seen the studio experiment with designs that take their large-scale creations beyond the gallery or conventional setting and places them in a public space, appearing spontaneously in laneways in Tokyo (Japan), Edinburgh (Scotland) and Melbourne (Australia). The pair will spend time sourcing native and seasonal materials in each city to create their designs, whether it's Japanese cherry blossom, Scottish thistle or Australian wattle.

In 2017 they created a ten-meter-by-ten-meter hanging installation made of wild asparagus plants for a public art festival in Spain.

Through the process of experimentation Wona and Charlie hope to better understand the relationship between humans and nature, which has been affected over time by the rapid increase in people moving to cities, leading to a disconnection from nature. By facilitating a meaningful reconnection with natural systems, the bond shared between humans and nature can be both strengthened and respected.

"We hope that through our work we can inspire people to interact and create with nature," says Wona. "We constantly seek to be surprised by nature and we are always experimenting and learning—this exploration is what drives us. Plants are not just decorative or stationary objects; they are complex systems that are mobile beings. We find nature truly fascinating."

◄ "Monstera Chandelier" created by Loose Leaf.
▲ Loose Leaf's Australian studio.

1. Loose Leaf is a botanical studio—how did you come to work in this field?

We love the irrational emotions nature evokes in us, and being able to create art using natural elements is a privilege. Through our creations we hope to enhance people's connection with nature. There is growing evidence that access to the natural environment improves health and well-being. We like to consider this when designing. Another unique benefit to our field is that we are lucky enough to witness people's reactions to our installations firsthand. We get to see the moment someone encounters our design for the first time. Design in our field can be incredibly gratifying both for us—the creators—and our audience.

2. Where do you draw your inspiration from?

We draw inspiration both from nature and the built environment. We love to highlight the interaction between both. There's something about sharing our botanical designs in a unique urban environment that makes them very easy to identify with.

3. What are some of your favorite designs?

We like to bring a playful energy to the designs we create. We often create opportunities for interactions between the audience and our installations. We're not sure if this makes them popular, but probably makes them more fun. One of our favorite designs for making this happen is the "Monstera Chandelier," a suspended ball of graphic greenery. We like to hang these at accessible heights where people can stand behind them and act like green monsters.

Lately we have been experimenting with designs that take our philosophy beyond the gallery or formal setting and into the public space. We recently tested this concept in Japan, Scotland, Australia, and Spain, where we created a series of interactive botanical installations both in the galleries and on the streets.

We have been experimenting with designs that take our philosophy beyond the gallery or formal setting and into the public space.

▲ ▲ ▼ Loose Leaf's sculptural art installations give people a connection to nature.

4. We noticed that some of your outdoor projects are so giant that you need to climb up and down to construct them. How does this affect your creative process?

We are fascinated by the idea of creating work that appears to defy the laws of gravity. Our mission is to incorporate methods of suspension that make our work appear as if it is floating. For this reason we're getting pretty good at travelling up and down ladders and scissor lifts.

5. You have been invited to create installations for many international events. Which one in particular has been a highlight?

We've had the privilege to create our installations for many top brands and events. Recently we were invited to Córdoba, Spain to create an installation as part of Festival Flora. We created a huge 10m x 10m hanging installation in the patio of a sixteenth-century palace. This was a surreal and inspiring environment to create our style of artwork.

6. You have published a book entitled *Loose Leaf*. What would you like to bring most to your readers via this book? Have you received any interesting feedback so far?

Our book, *Loose Leaf*, is about sharing our love of botany. It aims to encourage readers to get creative with nature. By sharing our designs and approach, we hope our readers find themselves taking in the greenery of the seasons and inviting nature into their own homes. Each section opens with an inspiring installation before guiding you through a small-scale project that you can try yourself.

We really enjoy seeing reactions to our book from around the world. We've seen some pretty interesting creations from our readers.

▲ Charlie, cutting wire mesh to arrange Monstera.
▼ "Post Bloom" installation.
▶ The Design Files "Collect" exhibition installation.

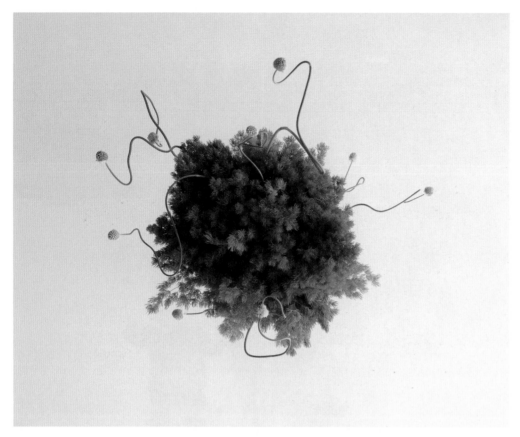

▲ ▼ Botanical installations created by Loose Leaf.
▶ Loose Leaf's "Free Fall" installation in Córdoba, Spain.

"We are fascinated by the idea of creating work that appears to defy the laws of gravity. Our mission is to incorporate methods of suspension that make our work appear as if it is floating."

Hover Arts

Floating Crafts

•

"I enjoy the challenge of different programs and personalities, and I enjoy the unexpected results gained from team work."

•

Josh Rosen

Commonly known as *Airplantman*, Josh Rosen is the man behind this brand. Infatuated with Tillandsia and other air plants, he set up his own business to give these living things what they need to thrive, and to highlight what is special about them. His hand-crafted works can be mounted as living art. His goal is to spotlight and maximize the extraordinary impact that air plants can have.

• **Occupation:** *Landscape architect, artist, and horticulturalist*
• **Location:** *Santa Monica, California, USA*

Growing up right next to the Raritan Canal, in New Jersey, Josh Rosen spent countless hours either running along the towpath or wandering in the woods. The contrasts of this beautiful landscape still inspire him. He is always amazed by the old, eroded locks that are used to control the water level because he loves the simplicity of their functional forms. The simple life here nurtures his passion for nature.

His story with air plants began with a trip to Hawaii, where he met many kinds of air plants and found himself completely absorbed by their extraterrestrial looks, independent habits, and their rich range of species, like the tiny and delicate duratii, the caput medusae with its odd sculptural form, and streptophylla, with its strange looks.

Surprised by the difficulty many people have keeping air plants alive, he decided to set up his own business, Airplantman, to celebrate this living sculpture. Josh is thought of as one of the pioneers who first introduced air plants to the public in an innovative way. He enjoys the moment when people look at his works with awed expressions. "Normally when people see plants, their brains don't pause, but keep working. We want to raise the cognitive dissonance: 'Wait, that's a plant, but it looks different and is floating in the air. What's going on here? I need to stop and learn more.'"

Josh has also created new products, like AirplantVessels and AirplantFrames, which not only provide enough sunlight and air to the plants, but also make their daily care and regular watering easier.

◄ Plants of various forms encircle Josh's studio.

▲ A wooden chair, a metal table, and steel frames help to present his air plant works.

▼ Pots of plants thriving on a table.

Apart from that, Josh has collaborated with many clients and created lots of large-scale projects. His designs are not merely dangling air plants hung by fishing wire, but thoughtful compositions. Josh and his clients spend countless hours debating every detail of the products and projects, striving to find the simplest yet most powerful solution to the problem. His favorite collaborations come about based not on drawings, sketches, or photos, but on mutual trust. Sometimes his clients are not able to imagine how a project will come out until it is completed, which gives him the opportunity to provide viewers with a chance to step back and connect with nature in a fresh way. "No one has ever been disappointed; it's just to make sure we have enough confidence to take the leap and move forward. The air plants themselves are easy to work with and usually very cooperative," says Josh.

Beyond daily work, Josh travels a lot. Not long ago, he joined a Tillandsia-focused eco-tour of Oaxaca and Chiapas in Mexico. For many years, Josh had been ordering boxes of Tillandsia from a nursery, so the moment when he found himself surrounded by plants in their natural habitat, he was excited and emotional. It was like visiting an old friend at their home for the first time, and it also helped his work from a scientific and practical perspective. He shared his experiences with film footage he shot and shared online. "I look forward to more trips in the future so that I can learn about the 'home' for different plants," says Josh.

◄ Josh arranging air plants in his yard.
▲ A large air plant frame hangs outside the Airplantman studio.

▲ This is where Josh usually seeks his inspiration and starts his creations.

▼ Completed AirplantFrames rest on the ground.

▲ Josh weaves air plants into a steel frame.

▼ Josh's passion, in a variety of forms.

1. How did you take your first steps in business?

My work as a landscape architect allows me to design outdoor spaces. As part of one of our projects, a client requested a living wall. I was fascinated by Tillandsia, and when I revealed a concept I had been playing around with at home, it led to funding to create a more refined version of my idea. The result was spectacular and I quickly realized this custom project could be made in large quantities and shared with the world. The rest has been keeping up with requests for new projects and keeping the online shop developing to meet the demand.

2. Your have created modern and minimalistic vertical gardens to display the charms of air plants. How did you come up with this concept?

Our goal was to create products that do three things: First, to highlight what is special about Tillandsia—that they grow floating in air and have unique and beautiful forms. Second, to make it easy to provide what Tillandsia need to thrive, which are air circulation and ease of watering. This is why our AirplantFrame is completely waterproof—to make submerging it along with its Tillandsias easy. Air plants don't love to be handled too often as our hands contain oils that are bad for their leaves. Products that allow you to water these plants without touching them lead to healthier, more beautiful plants. Third, we wanted to make products that are refined in their aesthetic so that the unique organic forms of the Tillandsia could really shine. We find beauty in the juxtaposition of nature's design with these plants and our human-made rectilinear forms.

3. We heard that you liked to collect plants when you studied in Chicago and that you even worked as an intern in a botanical garden. After that, you got your Master's degree in Landscape Architecture at the University of Arizona before you moved to LA. What have you learned in your previous roles?

"

My first step in my business was purely born of a passion for these plants and elevating their display.

"

◀ ▲ Outdoor scenery at Josh's studio.
▼ Frames on the tables inside the Airplantman studio.

It has been interesting living in such varied parts of the country. Each city had its own sense of place and a unique landscape. It's probably too much to share here, but in short I would say the experience of studying philosophy in college led me to seek connections to reality and this world, with an emphasis on the relationship between nature and people. I joked that after studying philosophy I wanted to stop talking about reality and start doing work where something would be undeniably different at the end. Landscape architecture is a profession where one shapes experiences and places and hopefully creates a relationship between people and nature that is mutually beneficial and increases the health of both. Practicing in LA over the past ten years as a landscape architect has provided countless fascinating experiences with people and places that have been both good and bad. In the future I hope to take these experiences and translate their lessons to create further changes to how we design, build, and develop policy that improves human lives and leads to healthier ecosystems. It's a tall order, but inspiring to try.

▲ AirplantVessels in glazed ceramic.
▼ Josh is creating his plant works.
➤ Rectangular AirplantFrames hanging on the wall.

4. What is your favorite thing about living with plants indoors?

It's hard to say—unfortunately I also live with cats who find plants far too tasty to simply admire from afar. While my garden and studio are overflowing with plants, no one remains alive and uneaten indoors!

5. You have customers from all over the world. Where do you see yourself going in the future?

I would love to do a world tour of all the amazing people we have connected with over the years and who enjoy our work. The response in Singapore, Australia, and Japan has been particularly strong and I would love to do a Pacific rim tour in the near future.

▲ ▼ ➤ Josh has collaborated with various customers and brands on large-scale projects.

"Our inspiration is often from clients who push us to
make their idea reality. With a little creativity and editing,
wonderful things emerge."

Floral

"Sweetness is a force. The balance between strength and fragility is what constitutes us, what constitutes the nature that surrounds us."

— *Claire Basler*

Retro Redolence

Encounter with Flowers

•

*"Find your own niche, be true to yourself
and stick to it. Always be acceptive of
adapting and change."*

•

Anna Potter

Anna Potter is the founder of Swallows & Damsons, a bustling flower
shop with an equally beautiful name in Sheffield, England. It is a
treasure trove of natural, seasonal flowers, rustic arrangements and
curiosities, which brings something distinctive to Sheffield. Inspired by
one of the best pieces of advice that she has ever received—*run your
own race*—Anna continuously searches for ways to express her unique
creativity.

• **Occupation:** *Owner of Swallows & Damsons*
• **Location:** *Sheffield, UK*

▲ Anna spends her time in a garden with clusters of colorful lupins.

After receiving her degree in Fine Art at Sheffield Hallam University, Anna Potter worked as a senior floral designer for two of Sheffield's leading florists. It was there where she realized what she truly wanted to be—a florist.

Exploding with creative ideas, she started Swallows & Damsons by selling flowers on the weekends at a beautiful chocolate shop. Shortly afterwards, she and her husband Dan bought an old office, which sits snugly between Jameson's Tearoom and an organic greengrocer on Abbeydale Road, in the heart of Sheffield's Antiques Quarter, and turned it into Swallows & Damsons. Talking about the shop's name, Anna says, "My favorite book as a child was 'Swallows and Amazons,' by Arthur Randsome, so the name of my shop was very much inspired by the book. It's a story about adventure, imagination and nature—these three things are now integral parts of our shop."

Anna has a passion for both vintage glamour and rustic styles, and she is determined to bring something distinctive to Sheffield. In Swallows & Damsons, a variety of ornaments form a perfect mixture of the vintage and the elegant—an array of old terracotta tea pots, natural history knick-knacks, and copper containers sit on the shelves, while the shop's mascot, a stuffed magpie called Margaret, perches on top of a nearby cupboard. "The flower shop was a huge challenge. When we first opened, the space looked like a 1980s office—stuffy, with strip lighting and crumbling ceiling tiles. The more we knocked down the walls and brought down the ceilings, the better we felt," says Anna.

Anna and Dan have collected all kinds of funky and distinctive objects from old buildings and second-hand shops, both in the UK and while traveling abroad. They then restored these aged objects, endowing them

▲ Rose gardens are where Anna normally picks flowers and finds her passion.

▼ Anna, arranging a bouquet in the greenhouse of Chatsworth House.

once again with vitality and color. They want to create a space that has character and adheres to the rules of simplicity, so as to let the things they love—mostly inherited and antique—shine.

Being obsessed with color, tone and texture, Anna's designs adhere to the formal rules of floristry. Depending on her customers' requirements, she adjusts the balance between flowers and space. Her work is a reflection of Western floral characteristics: dynamically rendered, colorful, mixed but not confused. Though her work adds romance to its spaces, Anna pays more attention to pragmatism—simple but above convention, elegant and with attentive details.

She often uses leftover flowers to create spontaneous and captivating art projects as well. By pairing those she cannot use in color-coordinated arrangements with different objects, she creates beautiful public displays.

For these projects she often chooses large, shaggy garden roses, which remind her of her nana's rose garden, where these stories all began.

Swallows & Damsons is enjoying growing popularity, through Instagram and coverage online and in books. Anna loves to share her ideas with fans, which, she believes, inspires her creativity. She also hosts a flower school in her shop where she offers floral arrangement lectures.

Along with her two sons, George and Albert, Anna likes spending time outdoors exploring Sheffield's countryside. Anna has a deep affection for this city, "I came to Sheffield as a student and quickly fell in love with the city, the countryside and its people. Sheffield has an industrial heritage which is still a key part of the city's architecture and design aesthetic. The beautiful conflict between the lush green fields and the dark brooding heather-covered hills inspires me daily."

◄ Anna uses Eremurus, poppy, Fritillaria, and Ranunculus to create her floral works.
▲ Anna decorates the staircase with spring flowers, which display their irresistible charms to visitors.

1. You have been running Swallows & Damsons for years. How and why did you choose to be a florist?

My flower journey really began when I was just a small child. We had a big garden growing up and my nana used to grow many different varieties of roses, which I enjoyed picking and making into perfume! I have been entranced with flowers ever since. I completed a degree in Fine Art and after that was fortunate enough to get a job at a floristry shop in Sheffield without having any experience. It was there where I realized floristry was the perfect fit for me. I worked with florists who had different styles but I eventually began to feel creatively frustrated. I wanted to work in a more natural, garden-oriented style, but there was nothing really around like that at the time. In 2008, I founded and opened Swallows & Damsons, where I create flowers in the style I love.

2. Do you still remember your first client?

We still see many of our first clients! For Swallows & Damsons, being a flower shop in the center of our community is at the heart of what we do. Having relationships with customers and making it easy for them to demonstrate their thoughtfulness is so important to us. It can be a challenge as having regular open hours is hard work, but it is a real honor to be a shop where people can reliably visit whenever they need flowers and to play a small part in the significant events in their lives.

3. You have made a bouquet for the Queen of the United Kingdom. How did you feel when you found out that your client was the Queen?

I was very nervous, as it was such an honor and privilege to be asked. We were informed of a last-minute outfit change, which meant we had to rethink our color scheme and design to stay coordinated, which was so much fun!

Working with a natural product means that there are different rules for each flower. No two stems are the same and therefore must each be handled in a different way.

◀ Heuchera leaves are the most frequent characters in Anna's works.

▲ Anna creating a bouquet in front of Dan's botanical paintings.

▼ Hand-made ceramics and pots fill the shop's shelves.

4. Where do you see Swallows & Damsons going in the future, in five years or so?

We hope to continue creating a brand that has an international creative influence, while remaining a local shop in the heart of the community—a family business with old-fashioned values.

5. You have collected many beautiful objects in your home. Is there a particular piece that means a lot to you? Have you always liked vintage styles?

The base of our shelving unit is an old pew that came from a gothic church built in 1817. All the pews were ripped out of the church and replaced with modern plastic chairs. Bringing the pews back to the shop gave both the pews and our shop a new lease on life. I've always loved antiques and curiosities, as they tell stories and hold a certain mystery about them. When I was a child, they would spark my imagination to dream up past lives and places. I love to have them as part of our shop. When children step into my shop, they are fascinated by the taxidermy, unusual artifacts and plants. It is a real hands-on experience.

6. We heard that your husband works as an illustrator. How did you meet each other?

We met at university when we studied Fine Art in Sheffield. Dan is the co-director of Swallows & Damsons and an incredible illustrator. He specializes in detailed botanical drawings, and insects and birds. He chose and arranged all the illustrations that are displayed on the feature wall behind our counter, which is one of my favorite parts of the shop's aesthetic.

7. Would you share with us some tips on how to care for flowers?

Keep it simple. Cool conditions and clean water.

▲ Hellebores lying casually on a book.
▼ Fallen petals are scattered around on the wood floor.
▶ Anna working on an arrangement.

▲ Chrysanthemums, dahlia, roses, zinnia, and seed heads harmonize in Anna's work, which can feel like an oil painting.

➤ An antique collector with Amaryllis, poppy, Ranunculus, Anemone, and roses.

"Working with unruly, delicate flowers and foliage is an utter delight, and instead of trying to manipulate them into a controlled design, we let the flowers lead. It's wonderful to let nature do its thing."

Bloom in Blush

A Scent from Nature

•

*"Sweetness is a force. The balance
between strength and fragility is what
constitutes us, what constitutes the nature
that surrounds us."*

•

Claire Basler

This legendary French artist is a painter of nature. Most of her works
focus on flowers and plants. Enamoured with the eighteenth-century
French arts, she has invented her own style of figurative art. Regarded
as one of the best examples of still life, it brings infinite inspiration to
other artists.

- **Occupation:** *Flower artist, painter*
- **Location:** *Château de Beauvoir, Échassières, France*

▲ Château de Beauvoir is surrounded by woodlands and meadows.

Claire Basler was born to an artistic father, who exposed her to art at a young age and inspired her to pursue it at École des Beaux Arts. After graduation she spent hours studying the masterpieces in the Louvre's collections, which provided further inspiration. The Louvre, she says, helped her to find her own way, and guided her to the door of her own artistic expression. With a sincere heart and an urgent need for freedom, she strengthened her resolve to become an artist.

Born in Vincennes in France, Claire Basler has shown great enthusiasm for exploring nature since childhood. Making the beauty of nature central to her work was, as she calls it, "a natural choice." Careful observation and a close connection with nature have brought her endless inspirations—the softness of a flower, the strength of a tree, the vaulted space of a forest, and the shocking openness of a meadow—all of these not only touch her soul, but enlighten her inner self.

Claire is fond of the eighteenth century's artistic aesthetic, but her work is quite different from the style of abstract and conceptual art that was popular in the 1980s, when she was developing her own aesthetic. She chose figurative art and integrated her own style into the still life to create vivid portraits. Though she was marginalized at the time, it never shook her belief. To this day, she continues to explore Mother Nature with the tips of her brushes.

▲ ▼ Beauvoir's walls are Claire's canvases where umbels and oriental poppies bloom. She creates her floral paintings in her home space.

In Claire's work, flowers do not compete with one another for attention. Instead, she offers in her work a subtle blend of the things she sees, the way she feels, and the thoughts she gains from nature. Every square-inch of color contributes to an understanding of the relationship between nature and human beings. She strives to reveal the mystery of flowers' life cycles—either blooming in the warm breeze of spring, or their rebellion against the chilly bise of winter. Life and vitality are the themes through her works, which not only restore the essence of living plants in their natural environment, but also narrate the cycle of life.

Claire lives with her husband Pierre in Château de Beauvoir, a thirteenth-century castle located in Échassières. She came across the castle on the Internet and fell in love with it immediately. She repaired the rooftop, laid the electrical circuitry, fenced a garden, decorated the furniture—everything was arranged and carried out step-by-step. She turned the walls into her canvases and filled them with blooming flowers.

Château de Beauvoir is quiet and far from cities, creating a calm, peaceful environment for Claire to create her work. From time to time, she holds open days for people to visit and buy her art. She feels lucky to be able to pursue painting. For her, this is definitely the best gift she has received from Mother Nature. "Joy is a tool of life and work. Joy and beauty are the sources of energy," says Claire.

◄ Nature is Claire's philosophy of existence.

▼ ▶ The dimension of her living space and her palette of colors define the Beauvoir's interior environment.

▲ Nature not only inspires Claire but provides her with freedom and confidence.

▶ Flowers and plants stretch from the tip of Claire's brush.

1. As a painter of nature, what do you love about your subject?

I love its sensuality. Its strength and softness. Its richness of emotions and inspirations. Its very fine and delicate colors. Its lights and shadows. The constant contrasts between life and death, presence and abandonment. Both in the figurative and proper sense. I have a limitless passion for this vital universe.

2. What was most challenging about the reconstruction of Beauvoir? How did you overcome it?

The beginning was difficult. We had a beautiful castle but there was no basic comfort here. And in winter, it is cold inside. Everything had to be done at once: installing electricity, tubing the huge chimney, repairing walls and windows, building a kitchen and a bathroom, etc. The castle is so big, which added more difficulties in the reconstruction. I started to paint the walls the first year and it helped us a lot. Life and sweetness have returned to the castle again. This has given us new strength and desire.

3. What inspiration do you draw from eighteenth-century art? How does it reflect in your art?

The seventeenth- and eighteenth-century French arts were my first influences. I loved the mysteries that spoke of the sweetness, freshness, fantasy, and power of these periods. It is difficult to summarize the whole feeling or philosophy towards paintings in words. There are multiple feelings—beyond the gloss of content itself, their impact comes from the way they were painted, the gestures of the painter, the palette of color and material and the intense emotion. I oppose the idea of an intellectual art—I prefer the domain of the sensate.

4. How do you like to interact with your viewers through your arts?

I am happy that everyone finds himself in my painting with his own feelings. It is a form of freedom shared between us. I don't want to impose anything, especially

I live in colors. I am charmed and surprised in all seasons by this endless game of colors. It is a very great happiness to be caught by so many colorful feelings, these gifts from nature.

▲ The harmony between painted flowers and nature.
◄ ▼ Claire likes to move the outdoor scenery into her creation of art works.

not ideas. I try to paint what touches me deeply and ignites me. It's like a daily breath, and the daily practice is very important. It is the regular observation of beauty.

5. Dreamy flowers melting in clouds and soft backgrounds are your signature style. When did this style come into being? Have you ever been influenced by other styles?

You translate the facts well. No, I was not influenced by other styles—I created this myself. I believe this is related to the happy moments in my childhood. This doesn't mean that I still want to be a child. My solitary journey has protected me from excesses in fashionability. Even though fashion is absolutely necessary for creativity and everyday life, it must not be devouring. Through this I found a timeless form of painting with a modern look. I'm not a ghost. I am very alive and nature speaks with me in a broad sense, not just as a subject of our spirit of domination. I can be a little daisy as well as a tree. I want to convey vitality. This is indeed in total opposition to the artistic period that I have lived through until now.

6. Do you have any advice for a new generation of artists for how to keep their own styles?

Freedom for artists is not about social status, but a big gift that is worth taking all risks.

7. For you, painting nature is a question of survival. Could you tell us more about this?

Life is a battle. Most of the oak's fruits would fall on the ground and few would survive. All my life I have identified with the little shoot as well as the big tree. Everyone must embrace their own existence, even when they are subjected to the unexpected—a storm or the growing greediness of the young. Life is like an equilibrist on a thread, resistant to rain, wind or burning sun on that fragile rope. Fighting and adapting. We must learn and accept. To accept is not to be defeated but to listen to one another. I would be invaded by my own doubts if I were not painting nature.

▲ Colorful paint brushes are Claire's working tools.
▼ Glorious blooms against a painted background.
▶ Claire's cat, examining her flowers.

▲ ▼ ➤ Various flowers flourish in Claire's oil paintings, including oriental poppies, Anemones, marigold flowers, and gold buttons. They represent hope, life, happiness, and possibilities.

"Humans have no more than nature, we just have means of different expressions, whether in our savagery or our quest for culture and civilization."

Crafting Colors

Exquisite Floral Wreaths

•

"There were lots of learning curves, and the making process itself is a constant learning curve."

•

Olga Prinku

Olga Prinku is a crafter and maker who uses embroidery hoops to create stunning floral works. Using both dried and freshly cut blooms, she creates artful and varied wreaths full of flowers, leaves, and berries. Her completed pieces not only display the charms of her floral materials, but also bring joy and love to her viewers.

~~~~~~~~~~~~~~~~~~~~~~~~~~~~~~~~

- **Occupation:** *Graphic designer, crafter, and maker*
- **Location:** *Yarm, UK*

Olga's work with floral wreaths began almost by accident. Previously, she knitted and sold woolen blankets, something she'd been working on for a long time. One day, during the Christmas season, she posted some photos of her Christmas stockings on Instagram to promote sales. To give the photos a festive touch, she added some Christmas wreaths to the scene. The wreaths were surprisingly well-received, and she kept receiving kind comments on them. This inspired her to start working on wreath-making, and later to move on to floral creation.

Instead of planning beforehand, Olga prefers to let her works unfold as she goes. Her elegant, creative designs begin with the materials of flowers, stitches, and gauze, but her working process depends on the complexity of the piece, which can convey anything from her personal and individual ideas about her life, her family, and the process of creating art with nature. The next step for Olga is to sell her artwork online, a significant challenge because her wreaths are very fragile. She has been experimenting with different types of packaging for safe shipping.

Currently, Olga shares tutorials about making floral creations through a YouTube channel. When asked about her intention behind her videos, she explains, "Partly it was because I was asked to teach a workshop and I am a very shy person when it comes to public speaking. I saw YouTube as a good way to try to get in some practice talking about my techniques.

◄ Magnolia in the living room, waiting to be planted outside.

▲ A clock wreath made of summer poppies in Olga's living room.

Also, I find it exciting when people get inspired by what I do and I'm always happy to be open about what I do and how I do it." Olga has enjoyed the power of her videos to bring together people with similar interests, who in some cases have become friends.

Olga regards her current work as a natural extension of her passion for graphic design. Her earlier career included stints at a small graphic design agency and an interior design magazine, experiences that have helped her to develop her sense of visual aesthetics. Beyond the final product, though, what Olga enjoys most is the creative process—coming up with new ideas and developing them through trial and error to see what she can achieve.

In addition to making floral arrangements, Olga is also keen on gardening as well as photography, a skill that helps her to capture and share images of her work.

◀ A eucalyptus Christmas garland above the dining table.
▲ Shelf details in the kitchen and a minimalist fern wreath.
▼ A knitted basket and flowers and berries on Olga's office desk.

▲ One of Olga's favorite hand-knitted rope baskets full of foraged hawthorn branches for crafting.

▼ Morning scene in the bedroom. For the festive season, Olga loves having a big bunch of red berries on the side table.

▲ A knitted blanket on a chair adds a leisurely atmosphere to Olga's house.

1. Most of your works are combinations of flowers, stitches, and gauze. What is it about this combination that appeals to you?

The answer is quite simple. I woke up one morning dreaming about this idea and I wanted to see if it was possible. I've done a bit of embroidery in the past and thought perhaps I could use an embroidery hoop to stretch the tulle fabric over, and then I could weave flowers into it. I've experimented with fresh flowers as well as the dried ones with different kinds of net-like structures, like a wrought-iron mesh table top, and different frames, like lampshades. Not all of these ideas work but you never know until you try.

2. Do you follow any principles when choosing flowers for your wreaths or hoops?

I love working with the seasons, so I tend to work on the principle of whatever is in season—I'll pick flowers and seed pods and whatever I can find locally, and dry them. Some flowers are more suitable for the embroidery hoops—it's best to choose flowers with thin stalks and heads that are not too big. Usually, when I choose flowers for a hoop, I'll pick some that share a certain color palette, whether it's pastel shades or bright colors.

3. What is the most difficult part for you when creating? What's the most interesting part?

The flowers are quite delicate and it seems that some days things all go smoothly, while on other days they keep snapping. I think it has to do with my state of mind—when I'm feeling calm and patient, things tend to go well, while if I start rushing then I make mistakes and I can get so frustrated that I have to walk away and do something else for a while. The most frustrating thing about breaking a flower is that there may not be an alternative replacement, so you have to rethink the whole design. The most interesting part for me is the excitement of seeing how the design comes together in the end because I don't have a plan before I start.

> *For me, nothing beats that feeling when you make something with your own hands.*

◄ Olga knitting a winter scarf in the studio.
▲ A knitting experiment using natural twine on big needles which eventually became a bag.
▼ The big loose knit meant Olga could experiment further and see how it would look with flowers weaved into it.

4. How long do your arrangements last?

There are two main things you have to do: try to minimise the amount of direct sunlight and the amount of moisture. So it wouldn't be a good idea to keep your flowers in a bathroom, for example. If you frame them and keep them behind glass, you can preserve them well and prevent them from gathering dust. Some flowers seem to last for longer and I'm learning as I go on.

5. You live in a quiet village and you mentioned that you're greatly inspired by the natural surroundings. What do you enjoy most about living with nature?

I enjoy having lots of walks nearby. As well as local walks around the village, we live not far from the moors and the coast so there are lots of opportunities to forage. Living in the countryside makes you stay in touch with the changing seasons. Even when I'm in the passenger seat of the car, I get inspiration from just looking out of the window and seeing what grows on the road.

6. You've said that you like to keep everything simple, which is reflected in your works and photos. Can you tell us more about your aesthetic?

My aesthetic is very minimalist—our décor at home is plain wood floors and white walls. Then I like to have some bright colors around as a contrast to that. I also love the textures of nature. Besides dried flowers and knitted wool, something I really enjoy creating with is the driftwood that I find at the coast.

▲ ▼ Olga combining grasses and seed pods to make a summer meadow wreath, with her collection of dried flowers.

➤ A memory book Olga likes to print each year with her favorite images.

▲ An embroidery hoop decorated with dried flowers became a giant wall clock.

▼ Autumn-inspired floral hoops.

➤ Flowers woven into a chair.

"I think you should define your own aims for what you want to achieve, as every individual is in a unique situation which will change over time."

Poetic Flora

Florist in a Glass House

•

"We consider all the details and we want to do more. Things do not exist, but we want to create."

•

Manuela Sosa Gianoni

Manuela Sosa Gianoni is the creator of GANG & THE WOOL, which is nestled in the Barcelona hilltops. Full of shimmering colors and rapturous scents, her glass crystal workshop is a paradise for flower enthusiasts. She integrates her love of floral creations into her work, caring for and working with these treasured blooms. Her philosophy synthesizes freedom and creativity, which extend well beyond her work.

• **Occupation:** *Owner of GANG & THE WOOL*
• **Location:** *Barcelona, Spain*

Manuela Sosa began her wanderings and adventures in Uruguay, where she was born and raised. But after attaining a degree in Fine Arts and Architecture, Manuela decided to move to Barcelona—a city that intrigues her with its pleasant weather, mountains and seaside, and wide range of cultures. Furthermore, the city has much to offer the artist, with its abundant raw materials and the company of other creative and restless people, some of whom Manuela worked with in design and exhibition production before she stepped into the floral world.

Manuela loves nature so much that she cannot imagine a life where she is not surrounded by pure air, mountains, and greenery. "Nature is certainly the greatest thing that we have as human beings. It's a task

for us to value her, take care of her, and to feel whole under the sky," says Manuela. Out of this deep love for nature and the strong urge to be part of it, Manuela started to add floral elements into her design works, until one day she suddenly realized that flowers had become the priority in her work. This is how GANG & THE WOOL came into being. GANG & THE WOOL is an exquisite flower brand founded by Manuela whose name might sound like it's a bit irrelevant to flowers. But Manuela established the brand when she was still working in the design field, and one of her goals was to create a name that carried more meanings. "I always find it interesting—a name that includes more things besides flowers, yet now flowers have become the fundamental material in our work," says Manuela.

◄ This little glass greenhouse is where Manuela spends most of her time—arranging flowers, holding events, etc.

▲ Flowers on a desk, waiting to be re-created.

▼ Manuela cutting flowers.

GANG & THE WOOL is located on a pastoral hill outside Barcelona. It not only serves as her studio but also her home. When she came up with the idea of building her own house, she aimed to create a multifunctional design that would be versatile enough to meet the needs of her personal life. Finally, she decided to construct a crystal glass greenhouse, which she had always dreamed about. GANG & THE WOOL was once dubbed one of the most beautiful flower shops in the world by *Vogue* (Spain). Nowadays, Manuela holds flower workshops, private meals, and photo sessions in GANG & THE WOOL. Her custom-made works have attracted many people seeking inspirations and collaborations.

In Manuela's floral arrangements, she usually combines fresh flowers from the world's largest market—Aalsmeer in the Netherlands—with Mediterranean materials she sources herself. She enjoys improvising bouquets, and in them she strives to feature the spontaneous character and nature of the flowers, rather than adhering to rigid structures and forms based on technical rules. She loves the beauty of imperfection.

For her, flowers are all different. Thus, when she creates a composition, she finds it imperative to watch how they bloom in a vase, and which places are suitable for them so that they fade in a natural fashion. She considers herself an artisan who is always curious about different creative fields. She explains: "Working with our hands is a natural way to give shape to ideas and be in contact with the material. I like to experiment and see what fits a certain space, what flower I should choose, which color or composition I should decide on."

Every morning, Manuela wakes up to the sound of birds chirping, prepares a delicate breakfast, and starts her work day in natural surroundings. She is happy to devote herself to what she loves and what makes her wake up with enthusiasm and passion. "Nothing is more beautiful than this, I suppose!" she says.

◄ ▲ Manuela uses a variety of colorful flowers to create different pots of bouquets, which decorate her greenhouse with liveliness and brilliance.

1. We hear that your affection for flowers comes from your mother's influence. Could you tell us about it?

My love for nature comes from my childhood. I grew up in a very natural environment. My father is a rancher in Uruguay and we spent all our seasons in the field. In addition, my mother knew how to transmit her passion for flowers. We spent hours in the garden. When we went to the countryside on weekends, she taught me not only the names of the flowers and her ways of caring for them, but also how to observe their leaves, stems, colors, and textures.

2. You have mentioned that you don't have a business plan for GANG & THE WOOL. How do you expect it to develop?

In terms of a business plan with profits and benefits, I don't have one. I'm the kind of person who tends to follow my heart, rather than reasoning. Right now, we're planning to offer our workshops in different countries, like in China, Japan, and Portugal. We hope that people there will be interested in meeting us and learning more about our philosophy.

We also want to experience the botanical beauty of each place and we'll work strictly with local materials to create botanical maps. In parallel, GANG & THE WOOL is a brand that aims to develop its own products and philosophy. Little by little, we're finding our collaborators and partners, creating home décor and accessories that speak for our individual identity and absolute respect for nature.

3. For you, what's the most enjoyable thing about living with flowers?

You have to feel them. It's very important to observe the flowers and combine them so as to transmit emotions— the passion and sensitivity of a piece of work. I am not a fan of excessive consumption and medals. I'm passionate about my job and that's what I wish to convey. I like the consistency in things. I think the creative eye is essential in all fields so sensibility is what I value most when selecting my assistants.

Flowers are 'precious' and recognized as a celebration of beauty. I feel lucky to work by their sides.

◄ Manuela doing some preparatory work for the coming workshop.
▲ Workshop participants enter a garden to source materials for the event.
▼ Pink and white colors create an atmosphere.

I'm quite radical and work many hours a day. It's hard to work in cold and hot weather because there are lots of pressures. But in this profession, effort, dedication, and hard work will give you the perfect result.

4. You're a florist, but at the same time, you're also an industrial designer, an art director, and a curator. How do you balance your time?

I love having these responsibilities. If I could start again, I would study exactly the same thing, only I would dedicate more years to it. What I appreciate most about participating in such creative careers is the feeling of seeing my projects develop part-by-part until they become coherent wholes, and reach their full potentials.

5. What do you think about the flower business?

Flowers now are just like tomatoes—they grow everywhere all the year round. It's incredible that in January we can have the same flowers sold at the same price as they would be in June. The floral world involves many people, but growers are disappearing. Excessive use of chemicals and fertilizers has led to dead flowers. It's a complex business—a daily struggle in which the overall effect is magical. I'm aware of these things and it seems very important to educate people to build a real world and cherish flowers.

6. You have a fondness for imperfection. Would you tell us more about it?

I love writing poetry that evokes our emotions for flowers. For me, nature creates the maximum expression of imperfection within perfection. Everything natural is perfectly imperfect. Because we're alive, we change and we move; the water flows and the snow melts; the leaves dry and fall. We all are part of nature.

⋀ Participants are encouraged to design their own bouquets.
⋁ ➤ Artful displays of local food add to the scenery.

▲ ▶ Manuela further expresses her love for flowers by working in portraiture.
▼ Comforting light shines through Manuela's works.

"The idea of building myself a foundation little-by-little fascinates me. Nature is the battery that makes my body work."

Indoor Garden

Nature on the Wall

•

"Be included in your work. Be generous with your knowledge. And be inspiring."

•

Hanna Wendelbo

Hanna Wendelbo has expertise in pattern-making. Her career in wallpaper began with a visit to a wallpaper store, which triggered a cascade of design concepts. Most of her works depict natural elements, like flowers, birds, and other living things. Before setting up her business, Hanna worked as a creative director, developing several award-winning projects for a variety of brands. Currently, she is one of the leading wallpaper designers in Sweden.

∿∿∿∿∿∿∿∿∿∿∿∿∿∿∿∿∿∿∿∿∿∿∿∿∿∿∿

- **Occupation:** *Wallpaper designer*
- **Location:** *Gothenburg, Sweden*

Hanna Wendelbo has had a close relationship with the natural world since her childhood, when she sought treasure in her parents' garden, and walked with her grandfather in his garden, listening to his stories about nature. Hanna's mother, a fabric enthusiast, kept a cupboard of beautiful textiles which Hanna enjoyed touching and feeling; her father ran an advertisement firm and always brought home nice pens, paper, and colors for Hanna and her sisters, encouraging them to draw and be creative. Influenced by her grandfather and parents, Hanna grew up with a strong passion for nature and design.

The turning point of her career path was an accidental encounter with a beautiful fabric shop located in an old bank office, which sold both wallpaper and fabrics. There was a big hall with a painted roof window in the middle of the shop, and the walls were decorated with dark wooden panels. Hanna was amazed. She instantly fell in love with wallpaper design and decided to work in the shop. Hanna exclaims, "I went to school, excited, and told my students about the wallpaper and my love for it. They thought I was crazy. But that excited me even more!"

◀ In the garden where Hanna finds most of her inspiration.

▲ A greenhouse allows Hanna to grow vegetables and flowers in Sweden's cool temperatures.

▼ Cosmea is one of Hanna's favorite flowers and grows everywhere in the garden.

After graduating with a degree in Graphic Design, Hanna worked at Sandberg Wallpaper for nine years and then spent five years at Borås Tapeter. With continuous creativity and endless ideas in mind, Hanna has created many well-received patterns. Eventually she became known as the "Wallpaper Queen" and is now one of the iconic wallpaper designers in Sweden. Despite her international fame, Hanna continues to work with care and diligence. "In wallpaper design, you can never be sloppy. One little mistake will be repeated, unchanged, over the full wall," says Hanna.

The pattern's repetition needs to be arranged with harmony of both form and color. Unlike poorly repeated patterns hidden in a piece of cloth, errors in repeating patterns on wallpaper can be easily spotted. This is a huge challenge that Hanna needs to conquer in her everyday work. Hanna has been to many different countries to learn and hold exhibitions. This frequent communication with the outside world has provided her with the opportunity to experience different cultures and to discover greater potentials within herself.

In 2017, with an inclination to try something new and an urge to slow down the busy schedule and spend more time with her family, she founded her own wallpaper brand in Sweden. Sweden, a beautiful country with epic and graceful natural scenery, is home to around ten million people. On the west coast lies Hanna's home, where she lives with her husband, three kids, a dog, and a rabbit. Most of the time she works at home, though sometimes she escapes to the nearby archipelago to relax. Hanna and her husband share a common passion for gardening, so they have built themselves a "secret paradise," where they can relax after work. She loves this garden so much that she jokes, "It's the only place on earth that I'm happy to claim as my own."

◄ ▼ ➤ The flowers in her garden bloom at different times, but pink and purple colors dominate throughout the season.

1. Flowers are the key element of your wallpaper patterns. What do you find special about flowers?

I love to work with flowers because they vary all the time. They might all look the same but if you take a closer look, they all bear their own personalities. Also, another compelling thing is that they won't last forever. Thus I try to draw them and turn them into part of my artwork. Colors in nature are always mixed in harmony, which is something that really makes my heart beat. I take reference from them to make lovely color schemes for my interior design products.

2. Apart from illustrations and wallpapers, you also create flower wreaths and mandala-like forms. How do you define your style?

I think my style is easy to grasp. I feel happy if my works can somehow inspire somebody to try making some floral works or to grab the brush and start painting watercolors. I think we all can exercise creativity in our daily lives. It's a sense of fulfillment.

3. Nature is the source of your creations and is conveyed through the theme of your artworks. Would you share with us your philosophy of living with nature?

In Sweden, we have at least five different seasons. In spring and summer, there is so much light and the sun never sets. In autumn and winter, it gets so dark and cold that you can't even imagine it unless you've been here. I live on the west coast where it barely snows to light up the long dull night. Sometimes we can go two weeks without seeing the sun at all. During the dark season, I try to design as many works as I can. It's pleasant to just stay indoors and paint and dream about the plans for my garden. When the sun returns in March, I'll get really busy with projects in the garden. The light also means new energy to me—when it comes, I never want to stay inside and sleep the day away. For me, living with nature means staying connected with it, enjoying the light, working in its rhythms, and embracing the seasons.

Colors in nature are always mixed in harmony, which is something that really makes my heart beat.

◄ ▲ ▼ Hanna draws and paints her wallpaper designs by hand. She likes working in both gouache and watercolors.

"MARGUERITE"
WALLPAPER DESIGN BY HANNA WENDELS

4. It seems that you have a deep affection for William Morris. Does he bring any inspiration to your creations?

Yes! Artwork during the English Arts and Crafts movement is a great source of inspiration for me. I think it's really interesting to hand-make great repetitive patterns. I also find a lot of inspiration in Josef Frank, an Austrian-Swedish pattern designer, best known for his big bold hand-drawn designs on fabric and wallpaper.

5. What do you expect the audience to receive from your works?

Happiness. When designing wallpaper, I hope that my quite naïve and mystic style will bring a warm and comfortable feeling to everyone's home. Wallpaper can last a long time, outliving trends. It is also my mission to try to inspire other people to be creative because it makes them feel so good. When sharing a film clip on Instagram, I aim to arouse people's interest so that someone might exclaim, "That looks so easy. I can do that myself!"

6. Where do you see yourself going in the future? In five years or so?

I only started my own business in 2017 but I've learned a lot about myself and my designing process. And it's so great to feel uplifted even though I had already worked in this industry for eighteen years. Hopefully, I can keep this feeling in the coming years as I know that my curiosity in this industry is still bursting. I hope I'll never feel that there's no more to learn.

▲ ▼ Wild strawberries begin as a sketch, above, and end up as a wallpaper design, below.

▲ Hanna begins illustrating for her new wallpaper collection, Morgongåva.

▼ Designs for "Vera" (left) and "August" (right).

▲ ➤ Flowers and nature are endless sources for Hanna's inspiration.

▼ An inky blue tone is the inspiration for Hanna's tissue paper design.

"Living with nature means staying connected with it, enjoying the light, working in its rhythms, and embracing the seasons."

Unsung Song

Forsaken Beauty

•

"Appreciating the beauty in things that often get overlooked is probably the single most important thing that guides my designs."

•

Fiona Pickles

Fiona Pickles of Firenza Floral Design is recognized as one of the leading floral designers in the UK. She can see beauty in the most ordinary details, which offer inspiration for her designs. Utterly infatuated with the seasons, she collects what is available in nature to create natural, grounded works. Internationally acclaimed and widely published, Fiona's work is instantly recognizable for its wild, untamed beauty.

~~~~~~

- **Occupation:** *Floral designer*
- **Location:** *West Yorkshire, UK*

Before pursuing her dream career as a florist and setting up her own business, Fiona Pickles worked in the printing industry, where her eyes learned to be sensitive to color.

She also spent two years working as a volunteer apprentice in a local flower shop, and the combination of the two experiences endowed her with the valuable skills and techniques to excel in her current job—florist and owner of Firenza Floral Design. Firenza specializes in weddings and events, aiming to make the whole process enjoyable and special—from the initial meetings with the clients, to the wedding ceremony where she can decorate the venues with flowers and deliver the bouquet on the morning of the wedding, and then the final cleaning and packing of all the rented items after the wedding ends.

Fiona's house and office are located in Halifax, overlooking the hills of West Yorkshire. This part of Yorkshire is also known as Brontë Country, named after the famous Brontë sisters, the writers who once lived there. "It's beautiful in an earthy, rugged way. Dark hills, brooding stones, steep hills, and craggy outcrops, all very *Wuthering Heights*! And I feel my designs are very much of this area. I don't really do 'pretty' or 'perfect' things. My work is very rugged, unstructured, and wild," says Fiona. She loves working with unusual color schemes throughout the year, often using brown, to make some of her works appear "dirty" or "withered." Fine and delicate color matching is what makes her work distinctive. She picks out a tiny touch of color from one single flower and blends it into another flower, and so on in a similar fashion, then matches the whole bouquet with a hand-picked

◀ Fiona working on some outdoor projects.
▲ ▼ Flowers in different forms are placed everywhere as interior décor in Fiona's house.

container to give a final touch to the whole design. Fiona was listed by *Vogue* and *The Telegraph* as one of the top twenty creative florists in the UK, a distinction she finds rather flattering. "It's so incredible to be recognized by two such influential publications," she says. "It still sounds pretty unreal!"

Deeply passionate about gardening, Fiona is happy to combine her love for growing flowers and designing. She is especially fond of scented flowers and herbs. To meet the huge demand for her flowers, she started growing her own, including tulips, roses, a few dahlias, and some annuals. It is liberating for her to wander around the garden and pick whatever strikes her fancy—she feels it is just like picking little stars from the sky—to go with her work, and make her designs distinctive.

Fiona's natural, relaxed style never fails to attract viewers. She is often asked by other florists to give lectures on how to polish their style while remaining unique and special. Each year she only conducts a few classes and workshops, which often include examples of her own artwork, such as large urns or installations. She also offers one-to-one tutorial classes at her home, which are a tremendous opportunity for those who aspire to work with natural elements. This is her favorite way to offer personal and special experiences in floral design.

Apart from flowers, three rescue dogs—Oscar, Ruby, and Flo—are also very important in Fiona's life, and occasionally appear in her Instagram posts. The dogs show up as she works, running and bouncing around the discarded rose stems or branches. Oscar can be very naughty, Fiona says, as he enjoys dropping his toys into the flower buckets, regardless of what is already inside. Sometimes the dogs blend right into Fiona's work because of their dark skin colors—the two whippets, who are actually grey, can shine blue in sunlight, while Oscar is brown. Regular dog walks enable Fiona to keep in touch with the beauty outside, inspiring her constantly with new aesthetics and nature's endless creativity.

◄ A wooden table and candlesticks add rustic touches to her home.

▲ ▼ Fiona is fond of using different ceramics with her flowers, from simple, handmade vases to large, unvarnished urns.

▲ Vintage ornaments evoke a sense of time.

▼ One of Fiona's whippets.

➤ Fiona's dogs are the important partners in her life—she loves being surrounded by them after work.

1. Firenza Flowers is named after your grandmother, Florence. Would you tell us more about it?

Naming the business was something I deliberated about long and hard. I toyed with all sorts of options but I always knew I wanted it to be personal and what would be better than to name it after a family member? I actually had a few options to choose from—my maternal grandmother's name was Florence, and she was known to everyone as Flo; my paternal grandmother's name was Olive and my maiden name is Wilde—rather appropriate! But I eventually decided to settle on Firenza, a twist on the Italian for Florence. I know it sounds a little strange but I just love the letter "Z" in the word. Since its establishment in 2005, my business has gone through many transformations and I now feel my work is akin to floral art and I love that the city of Florence is so closely associated with art. It feels so appropriate.

I feel now I have come back to where my heart lies and am totally in my element.

2. Your works are natural and relaxed. How did you develop this style?

When I first started the business, I worked with ingredients from my garden, but this was mostly unheard of at that time and I worried that it would be viewed as somehow "lesser" and "unprofessional." So I moved away from that and did what would probably be described as traditional wedding floristry. Much as I loved working on so many beautiful weddings, it was different from my natural style. I don't regret but I do wish that I had carried on with what I started initially. If I could offer one piece of advice to anyone starting out, it would be: Don't worry about what other people may think and just follow your heart. I feel now I have come back to where my heart lies and am totally in my element.

3. Your works depend on the seasons. Would you tell us more about this?

There is a reason why things happen in nature. Tiny flowers on the woodland floor bloom early in the spring before the trees develop their light-obscuring canopies. Fruit trees bloom early to give time for fruits

◄ Fiona picking flowers in her garden.

▲ ▼ In her studio Fiona chooses varieties, cuts the branches, and arranges the flowers. She holds classes here sometimes.

to develop later in the season. Foliage changes to all sorts of amazing colors in autumn before the leaves are shed and trees get ready for winter preparation. Why don't we work with this natural beauty and embrace the hellebores, forget-me-nots, fritillaries, and tulips in spring and deep earthy, rusty colors of flowers and foliage in autumn?

4. You are a leading advocate for British flowers. Where does your passion come from?

I started working with British flowers in large quantities back in 2013 and have met so many amazing growers who grow a huge array of enticing, unusual, and interesting flowers. I'm so pleased to see the huge growth in their popularity. Locally grown flowers are so interesting. They have life and personality and can create the most beautiful shapes and structures. They are the final little flourishes that would lift a design to something amazing. Using British flowers is very different from buying flowers from the huge, efficient Dutch machine and it requires a different way of thinking. But it's something I will always do for the sake of the beauty of flowers.

5. You are very keen on capturing the beauty of life. Would you share with us your aesthetic?

Appreciating the beauty in things that often get overlooked is probably the most important thing that guides my designs: a drying hydrangea head with skeletonised petals showing an immense beauty, a contorted stem of jasmine trailing around and creating incredible shapes, a twig covered in lichen, and ferns giving out amazing colors of coral, amber, and brown. If you left me in a beautiful garden filled with vivid flowers, I would give up all these and work with the overlooked, understated pieces. They are the unsung heroes!

▲ Flower cuttings scattered on a desk.
▼ Roses in an earthenware container waiting to be used.
➤ Different ceramics add to the unique feel of Fiona's studio.

▲ ▼ ➤ Fiona's specialty is big outdoor projects, especially for weddings. She uses seasonal flowers and matches them together to highlight their natural beauty.

"My designs are totally grounded in both the surroundings and the seasons and are totally representative of me and what makes my heart sing."

Miniature

"There are many ways that living species communicate. To be able to communicate with them, we have to learn how to be silent and to listen."

— Fem Güçlütürk

Imaginary Factory
A Cactus Collection

•

"Always be true to yourself and your concept. We have followed our dream and have had so much fun reaching it. It's very important to find a focus and stick to it."

•

Maja, Cille and Gro

In the hustle and bustle of magical Jægersborggade, a street in the riotous-turned-hip Nørrebro district in Copenhagen, there is a tiny space filled with cacti and succulents. Kaktus København is a concept shop run by three women: Maja, Cille, and Gro. Its Scandinavian style of cacti has brought new vitality and dynamicism to the plant industry.

· ·

- **Occupation:** *Owners of Kaktus København*
- **Location:** *Copenhagen, Denmark*

▲ The front door of the Kaktus shop at Jægersborggade 35, Nørrebro, Copenhagen.

Having grown up in the countryside, sisters Maja and Gro and their closest friend Cille have had an indissoluble bond with cacti since they were children. They took gardening classes together, and their parents always kept collections of succulents around their houses. Sometimes they were even wakened up by their parents in the middle of the night to see a cactus's flowering, which was rare to see in the daytime. Driven by their admiration and fascination for the prickly, introverted, and artful works of nature, Maja, Cille and Gro opened Kaktus København in Copenhagen in 2015.

Kaktus is a little shop decorated in a minimalist style with the use of soft yet unique colors, which shows the owners' delicate aesthetics and distinctive taste. Unlike other traditional plant shops, Kaktus is a shop that sells more than 150 different exclusive Danish-grown cacti and items designed from plants. To make original art pieces out of succulents and pots, the three young women collaborate with both international and local ceramic designers.

Along Jægersborggade stand several unique shops, selling caramels, nitrogen-frozen ice cream, and the best coffee in town, not to mention art galleries, organic bakeries, a mushroom farm, a tattoo shop, vegan burger joints, and many others. With so many concept stores around to provide them with daily inspiration, Maja, Cille, and Gro are always in search of experimental projects and collaborations. This is how they came up with the edible cactus jam and

▲ The shop's interior.

▼ A Kaktus tote bag with the shop's logo (left) and the shop's highlight (right), the hanging "planteplanetere," made by Kaja Skytte.

syrup made out of the fresh opuntia cactus. To the jam they add a very traditional Nordic ingredient—the sea buckthorn—to create a flavor to excite the taste buds. Besides using cacti as an ingredient in new recipes, they often hold various artistic cactus-themed events, like drawing and printmaking workshops.

Maja, Gro, and Cille may sound like an odd combination—by training, Maja is a retail designer, Gro a sociologist, and Cille an urban planner. But together they bring new perspectives to the plant industry. Despite their differences, they perform their roles in Kaktus, and their minds are very much aligned. "Sometimes one of us gets a new idea and can't wait to share it, and when she does, it turns out that we are of the same mind. We all have very creative minds and have a straight and honest way of running a business." The three always strive for things that are fun and vigorous. "Sometimes we might have to wake up at four in the morning and load a van in the rain for hours—very exhausting. But when we look around, we know that we each have two best friends standing by! And then we finish the chores together with happiness and joy," they say, laughing. For them, running a shop in the city is full of daily challenges. The biggest challenge, they feel, was convincing people around them that they could open a shop for selling succulents only, no matter how crazy the idea sounded. "Our biggest challenge ended up being our best decision," they exclaim.

◄ Scandinavian aesthetics inform the shop's displays.
▲ Cecilie Krawack in the shop. Picture by Gro Magazine.
▼ Woodchips and cacti on display in the Kaktus shop. Picture by Gro Magazine.

1. Many people believe that cacti are a perfect fit for Scandinavian style of simplicity. What do you think of that?

Our primary focus in opening this cactus concept store was to show people that cacti, generally known as arid plants, can fit into the Nordic lifestyle. Scandinavian style is known for its simplicity, and we think that the cactus's aesthetic suits this perfectly. We like to see cacti as green sculptures. Compared to leafy green plants, cacti grow up slowly, so you can keep them as small decoration items in your home.

2. Where do you usually go hunting for the plants or ceramics?

We don't go to the big plant markets. Instead, we work with Danish and local cactus farmers who have local greenhouses. It's important for us to know where the cacti come from. We once found a fifty-eight-year-old cactus at a greenhouse, and you can imagine how excited we were. We moved this cactus to our store, but we learned about its past from that greenhouse. Cacti can have a long lifespan, so we believe that they carry great stories. We get pots from the local ceramic shop, and they are all handmade. When you put a beautifully shaped cactus into a handmade ceramic pot, it becomes a small art piece. It's a way for us to interpret and display nature.

3. København is your hometown. It's also your store's name. You've said that your inspiration comes from this city. Could you tell us more about this?

Yes, Kaktus København is named after the city we live in. The aesthetic of the store and our visual identity are inspired by the town and the people who live here. We love the district of Nørrebro, which is primarily known for its small unique businesses and laid-back vibes. Our shop is also a place for people to come and hang out for cacti and coffee. We used elementary and light Scandinavian materials when designing our shop. So for us, it was essential to get some København aesthetic into our shop design.

We can't deny that København is a big part of our identity; we simply love the city and its vibe.

◀ A Euphorbia cactus.

▲ The shop's outdoor summertime display in Torvehallrne, in the center of Copenhagen.

▼ Assorted cacti on a wooden shelf.

4. You haven't been formally trained as botanical designers. Does this affect your work?

We think of not having educational backgrounds in botany as a strength. We aren't gardeners or plant experts. We once spent three days interning in a traditional flower shop, and we won't say that this wasn't a useful experience, but after the three-day internship, when we were asked to create traditional Valentine's Day decorations, we simply left the shop and went straight to a forest nearby. Breaking through tradition enables us to bring some fascinating and new ideas to the whole plant industry. Why do we give red roses on Valentine's Day when we can send an everlasting cactus instead?

5. What are your plans for your shop?

▲ ▼ Graptopetalum bellum (above) and Euphorbia ferox (below).
➤ Cacti on display.

We have always taken one step at a time with the cactus project and we've felt very honored to be able to run our shop for three years now. Our mission is to constantly develop our concept shop and expand the universe of cacti that we have created so far. Our shop has also turned into a "nerdy" place—it's the go-to place if you are looking for a particular rare cactus or succulent spices. Now you can even buy a cactus in the supermarket at a very low price, but you can't get a rare or weird one, like a sixty-year-old cactus, for instance. So we work very hard to present a unique collection of cacti and handpick each plant to make sure only the best come into our store. So in the future, we want to keep on being the very best cactus store and to inspire more people to live with plants.

6. Could you share us some cacti-care tips?

Cacti love sunlight. The best place to keep them is a window spot or in a bright room where lots of light shines in. Too much water is the biggest enemy to cacti. Let the soil dry totally out in between the watering. A trick is to use a little wooden stick or a pencil and put it in the soil before watering. If there is soil on the stick and it seems wet, then wait another week to water.

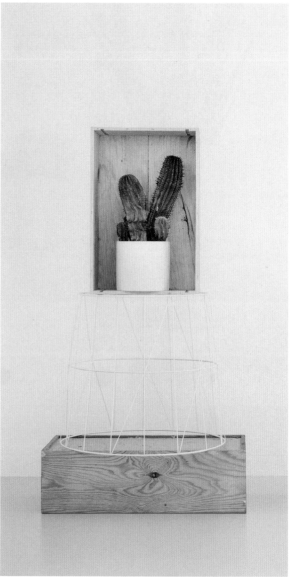

▲ Kaktus also features creative ceramics, which here present striking presentations of Pachyphytum hookeri and Euphorbia.

➤ A portrait of Euphorbia trigona f. rubra, Ferocactus stainesii, and Opuntia violacea.

"We all share the same passion for cacti, and we like to get our hands dirty and enjoy a conceptual way of working with plants."

Antonio Jotta and Carol Nóbrega

Urban Jungle
A Scent of Greenery

•

"Nature is a labor of love, and there is no room for hatred. We'd like to spread love with what we do and open people's eyes to all the magic that surrounds us on a daily basis."

•

Antonio Jotta and Carol Nóbrega

FLO Atelier Botânico is a store that brings nature back into our daily lives. With exotic plants, all sorts of miniature, oddly-shaped yet charming terrariums, as well as beautiful vases and ceramics, Antonio and Carol have infused beautiful design and wild nature into FLO. FLO is also known as Oasis Urbano, which translates to English as "Urban Forest." People are intrigued to come for a special visit and to see how amazing nature can be. It is a place that reveals the botanical world and serves as a space for events and workshops.

••

• **Occupation:** *Shop owners*
• **Location:** *São Paulo, Brazil*

FLO Atelier Botânico is a botanical store in São Paulo established by Antonio Jotta and Carol Nóbrega. It is named after the film *For Lovers Only*, because Antonio and Carol both embrace true romance and wildness at heart, and they regard the shop as the offspring of a love story between design and nature. The idea of founding such a botanical store was initially derived from their trip to Paris. Antonio and Carol were obsessed with the floristry in Paris, which has a mysterious beauty. Inspired by these unconventional florists, they decided to open their store.

The shop looks like a greenhouse with white walls, a cold gray floor, and half-glass rooftops, which let in plenty of sunlight to the room. Steel frames create geometric lines in the air and plants are placed or hung around casually to adorn the clean space. The result is harmony between natural wildness and modern design.

On the shopping bags reads FLO's slogan, *A Natureza Dentro de Casa*, which translates to English as "Nature Inside Your Home." This is also the spirit that FLO strives to convey. The shop is well-received by the locals and in September 2017, Antonio and Carol expanded with a second shop just two blocks away from FLO.

Antonio and Carol believe that being in touch with nature goes much further than just keeping plants in one's living room, so apart from succulents, they curate and promote items like candles, pots, and aromatherapy in their shop. They hold the view that it is important to find moments of calmness in one's busy life, and nature can help. "For example, lighting a scented candle made from lavender and chamomile essential oils is the perfect way to create a peaceful atmosphere and to care for your wellness."

◄ A view of the shop looking fresh and ready in 2016 for Antonio and Carol's spring installation, where friends and visitors were invited to pause a moment and take all the colors in and be touched by the power of nature.

▲ A shot of the shop on the day FLO opened its first installation, which aims to reconnect people with nature.

The duo run their business in an atypical way. Although they love their jobs, they have their share of problems to deal with. It is tough for them to maintain everything in order in the shop. Sometimes they even joke their workday is like a chef's day, as they need to deal with perishable items. Everything must be done on schedule or the whole operation falls apart.

Outside of work, Antonio, Carol, and Frida, their dog, live together and form a happy family. They like to travel and experience new circumstances, which open them to diverse perspectives. The three all play their roles in this family: Antonio is a Renaissance man who embraces the belief that people are limitless in their abilities; Carol is "the soul of FLO," and Frida is "the inspiration muse." "Even though we have different aesthetic views, expertises, and personalities, together we find what works best for each case. As in nature, diversity makes all the difference," says Carol.

For the future, this couple says, "We would love to take FLO to a new country and share our passion with a new community! Not only do we curate design items focused on plants, but also aim to expose nature's design. There are no concrete plans right now, but we are open to new possibilities."

◄ A different angle from the same day they celebrated the beginning of spring.

▲ ▼ Antonio and Carol's love for cacti is no secret. Here they paired some of their favorite species with crystals in terracotta pots and in terrariums.

▲ Curated goods for botany lovers.

➤ In FLO, you can find inspiring books on designing with plants and flowers, vases, tools and your very own miniature garden.

▲ Miniature desert gardens (left) and succulents planted in a reclaimed wooden box Antonio and Carol designed (right).

1. Your shop sells many specimens planted in glassware instead of in traditional pots. Why do you feature terrariums?

Even though we also sell traditional pots, we started and grew with terrariums. We were very intrigued by the Victorian style of bringing plants indoors in containers and started researching more about it. The fact is, most people don't spend a lot of time at home and therefore they can't care for their plants on a daily basis. Terrariums are easier options, and they are basically miniature gardens. Even those who live in small apartments can have one. We believe that everyone can be more in touch with nature, and limitations of space or time shouldn't be a problem anymore.

2. Have you ever run out of inspiration while creating your works? How do you maintain your creativity?

Oh, that's a great question! And yes, such situations happen, especially when your business grows and you have to deal with so many tasks. When we realized that we were getting into a routine that wasn't very inspiring, we decided that we would create a themed botanical installation twice yearly, to inspire our new designs and products. We get very excited about planning these! Other than that, we are huge plant nerds and love to travel. You can always spot us at botanical gardens, natural history museums, plant nurseries or even just appreciating people's gardens.

3. FLO holds forums on various topics. What do you discuss most frequently? What would you like to bring to the public through these forums?

We promote workshops so that people can have the opportunity to learn how to make terrariums, kokedamas, and other botanical creations with us. We also occasionally host talks to demystify some beliefs about plants. Many people are hurt because they "killed" their plants and are worried that they won't be able to help a plant thrive. It all comes down to reconnecting people with nature.

Studying your craft is extremely important—we have done so and continue to but not in the traditional way.

◄ This beautiful frame is from the Danish brand Moebe and is a perfect way to exhibit dried specimens.

▲ Strange plants are Antonio and Carol's big passion. This bonsai of a schefflera had them in such awe that they eventually added it to their personal collection.

▼ Carol styling the air plants. They occasionally refer to this species as "aliens" because of its strange looks.

4. Carol, you've mentioned that the art and aesthetics of the 1920s have inspired you a great deal. Could you tell us more about your preference for this era?

I am interested in vintage botanical illustrations and have a vast collection of these images. I love how faithful they are to nature and all the textures and movements involved. It is something that I apply to my designs. Rather than making an arrangement stiff, I prioritize the stem's natural movement and seek to show the plants' uniqueness. Even earlier than the 1920s, the Victorian era is a huge inspiration. They brought the outdoors in and became obsessed with the wonders of the botanical world. Keep in mind that at this time, so many plants were complete novelties in Europe, as they were being brought in for the first time from the so-called "New World."

5. Could you tell us something about your daily life in São Paulo?

As in other large cities, life in São Paulo can be very intense. We work in the typical chaotic scene but we have constructed a peaceful life. Our home is very close to our workplace and is situated in a neighborhood with a lot of greenery, so we rarely suffer from a big traffic jam or complain about it. What we love about this city is that there is always something new happening and so many creative people are having their voices heard.

▲ In the terrarium workshop, students get started with the plants.

▼ Cacti are ready to move into their new home.

➤ Antonio and Carol have repurposed this vintage cabinet with air plants and marimo moss balls in lab containers.

▲ A collection of terrariums Antonio and Carol have designed over the years. The background is one of the botanical wallpapers they created for Branco.

▼ Closer inside to admire how diverse nature is.

➤ The green edges of this succulent have turned into an amazing burgundy tone.

"Our wish is to inspire and reconnect our visitors with nature. Sharing our passion and seeing how people react to it is so rewarding."

LUNDI FERMÉ
MARDI 11:30-19:30
MERCREDI 11:30-19:30
JEUDI 11:30-19:30
VENDREDI 11:30-19:30
SAMEDI 11:30-19:30
DIMANCHE 11:30-18:00

Terrarium World
Life in Miniature

•

"I love the constant surprise and the endless possibilities of how a plant will turn out to grow on its own."

•

Noam Levy

Paris, the cultural heart of the nation that gives us the *Jardin à la Française*, is where Noam Levy and his miniature paradise Green Factory can be found. Green Factory is a store dedicated to producing beautiful terrariums that can generate the conditions to sustain themselves and only need a few fluid ounces of water a year. These plants, which are almost effortless to grow, are an excellent choice for those who are eager to live with greenery but have limited time and budgets.

• **Occupation:** *Founder of Green Factory*
• **Location:** *Paris, France*

Noam Levy has been in love with gardening since his childhood. As a boy, he loved having his hands in the dirt, collecting cuttings, testing various soils and species, and waiting for the seeds to sprout. Always an enthusiastic plant lover and collector, Noam dreamed of owning a plant shop. In his thirties, he finally decided to jump into entrepreneurship and he opened Green Factory. He found that ficuses and ferns can remove pollutants from the air, so he started focusing on the beauty of plants and the pleasant environment they create. After experimenting and sourcing for years, he finally found the best plants for a full moist environment, which would become the featured plants in his terrariums. Green Factory is a place where Noam makes his dream a reality. Recalling his favorite moment working with plants, Noam says, "I love the constant surprise and the endless possibilities of how a plant will turn out to grow on its own."

◄ The front door of the Green Factory.

▲ Noam and Anna searching for new inspirations.

▼ Glass terrariums with different themes are displayed on shelves.

Noam's terrariums are the embodiments of forests and prairies, and pleasant to the eyes. Each of his terrariums can hold about fifteen different plants. Most of his miniature works favor moist environments. At the bottom of each glass is a drainage layer made of volcanic gravel that represents groundwater. The plants send their roots down to collect the condensed water that drips down along the glass walls. Above the volcanic gravel are layers of finer gravels and sand to facilitate drainage, and above those are the sedimentary layers and the soil. Noam optimizes these unique three-layered blends to suit both plants and miniature trees.

Noam's terrariums are like mini green worlds with various themes, unique yet coherent with each other. Before setting up Green Factory, Noam spent a year in Israel learning how to plant, to sow, and to irrigate in poor soil and dry environments. He also traveled to many other countries including India, Australia,

Thailand, and Brazil. All these journeys led him to where he is now. "What I brought with me from those journeys is inspiration, mostly. I got inspiration from the fantastic landscapes and trees I saw and from my many encounters. My work is to create little worlds, so it's a big help for me to see different sides of our world."

After learning from countless mistakes, Noam has compiled a list of best practices for creating a terrarium. For example, one should be careful about the size of the plants and be prepared for them to expand over the years. Plants and moss that will compete with one another or occupy too much space cannot be placed in the same terrarium, and plants with different environmental requirements should not be combined. As a botanical designer, Noam does not merely design plants, but also researches and teaches people how plants can benefit life in the city, one of the central goals for Green Factory.

◄ ▲ ▼ Noam and Anna are working on a new terrarium project by following the principles of placing the gravel, sand, plant, and soil step-by-step.

◀ ▲ Working with plants is the happiest pastime for Noam and Anna.
Each of the terrarium works has its own theme, and looks like a real living green world.

1. Your miniature works are self-sufficient. That sounds incredible! How did you come up with this idea?

The idea dates back to the early 1830s with the discovery by an English botanist, Nathaniel Ward, who found that a sealed terrarium will thrive. Most terrariums were composed of ferns or low palm trees at that time. They were first popular in Victorian Era, and then throughout the West by the 1960s. In 2013, I tried to renew this fantastic idea. I came up with what you see today by adding leafy trees and moss to the arrangements, which now are an important part of miniature landscaping. Today, I'm still exploring new possibilities. Nature and the life cycle in our world, including photosynthesis and water circulation, are what make these little jars work. It's incredible that there is enough oxygen in the jars to sustain life. These terrariums share the same great mechanisms as the Earth, allowing the plants to thrive.

2. What do you think are the advantages of selling handmade works and what challenges do you face?

Most items sold nowadays are mass-produced objects, identical to one another. I see each work as a unique landscape. It is like a garden that takes one's time and energy to maintain. The primary challenge is the budget, especially in a city with such a high cost-of-living. Another major problem is explaining to clients the price of handmade items and the originality behind them. Most customers understand this, and we try to provide them something genuinely original at an affordable price.

3. Some people call your place Paris's "best-kept secret." How do you feel about that?

It all started in the early spring of 2014 when I rented a run-down shop to fill my orders and to experiment on new projects. Later I had unexpected visitors—curious residents from the neighborhood would look through the window, and others would step in to ask

What I loved the most was the experiments. I would just do it and wait for it to thrive or wither.

me questions and show great interest in the mini-worlds I was making. That was my first victory and also the pivotal moment when I decided to turn it into a terrarium shop. By then, Green Factory was no longer a one-man job, and my partner Anna had joined the adventure.

In the first few months, we made our plant arrangements on a big central table and placed them on the side shelves. I brought in new glassware every other day to experiment with terrariums. The more we were creating, the more curious people came in, which gradually turned into some business. Now the Factory has grown into a company with twenty-five employees, and I celebrate its achievements every day.

4. Do you have any plans for the Green Factory, over the next five years or so?

I believe we are on a great path of expansion. If you had told me two years ago that we would sell our terrariums in prestigious venues all over Europe like The Conran Shop and Selfridges in London, Le Bon Marché in Paris, and Kadewe in Berlin, or in places as far as Hong Kong, I wouldn't have believed you!

5. Do you have any suggestions for beginners?

I would recommend they choose plants that will thrive in the environment where they live and with the amount of time that they will spend taking care of them. I have heard people saying, "I could even kill a cactus." They either overwater the cactus, fail to provide them with proper light, or place them in a pot without adequate drainage. It's not necessarily hard to care for a plant, and the best thing is to start with where you will place them and make sure the humidity requirement is taken into account. Even though your schedule might be frantic and you barely have time to spare, you should squeeze in a moment to water it, trim a few branches or clean its leaves.

▲ A Pilea awaits transplanting.
▼ ➤ Glasses filled with miniatures are the central decorations in Green Factory.

▲ ▼ ➤ Pots of plant works.

"My first victory was managing to make Parisians, who are busy with their hectic lives, enter the store, even though I had no intention of selling them things."

Jennifer Tao

Bohemian Gems

A Plant Gatherer

•

"I enjoy living in a room filled with the things I love."

•

Jennifer Tao

Jennifer Tao runs an online store selling succulent products and spreading her love for plants to people worldwide. Having grown up in Southern California, Jennifer appreciates nature and gets inspiration from the surroundings. She doesn't have much of a green thumb, but she finally discovered that succulents are the perfect match for her. By selling a vast collection of succulents and exquisite handmade plant adornments, she is quickly gaining popularity online.

• **Occupation:** *Succulent enthusiast*
• **Location:** *Camarillo, California, USA*

According to the records, data shows that California has been stricken heavily by one of the worst droughts in the past few years. To conserve water, the authorities began to encourage the locals to reduce usage and grow more drought-tolerant plants to improve the urban landscape. Following this trend, Jennifer Tao started her study of succulents. Greatly awed by these magical plants—varieties that can grow from just a tiny leaf, with little care—Jennifer began collecting her succulents from the local shops and large wholesale growers, and even as presents from her friends. She built a plant garden in her front yard and tends it with joy and love.

Living on the Pacific coast where the local climate and other geographical factors are suitable for succulents, Jennifer planted a variety of them in her garden without worrying about whether it gets too hot or too cold. "I always say that this place gives me an unfair advantage because I don't need to toil so much. I let them thrive on their own continuously."

Besides cultivating, Jennifer has also developed many creative works with succulents, like the pieces in her dreamcatcher series, which are made with living succulents, and which come out beautifully thanks to her hard work and great care. Jennifer recalls that in the beginning, she was worried about turning what she loves into a job because she did not want the stress to take away her enjoyment. Fortunately, with the help of her friend, Becca Stevens, she went on, without hesitation, and started to sell their succulent objects in their online shop, Botanical Bright. "It's a wonderful thing to be able to share something made with so much love with so many people," Jennifer says.

◄ Jennifer removing cuttings from her front garden to create room for new plants.

▲ Part of Jennifer's succulent garden in different colors with large stepping stones.

▼ Close-up view of Jennifer's garden and a beautiful cluster of Aeonium.

Being a fan of the retro-bohemian style, Jennifer decorates her house with a lot of delicate ornaments, like crystal stones, macrame, candles, etc. Without any specific rules for the decorations, the house looks so eclectic, colorful, bright, and organic that it becomes a calm and peaceful space where Jennifer can get inspiration and ideas. "Houseplants can purify the air in a completely natural way; crystals can beautify the space and bring energy to the home. I enjoy living in a room filled with the things I love," says Jennifer.

Jennifer works in the mornings and in the afternoons she picks up her son, Josh, from school and tries to spend time doing fun things outdoors with him. They love going to the beach for relaxation. "Spending time on the beach has always helped me keep positive on things. It's hard to have a bad day or to feel sorry for yourself when you're standing on the shore, looking into the beauty and vastness of the sea. I feel humble in front of the ocean when I realize how strong and powerful it is," says Jennifer. Thus, she reminds herself to stay composed and optimistic whenever she comes across a problem. With Jennifer's influence, Josh loves to plant things and feels proud when he sees things start to grow. He is always asking Jennifer to buy him new plants, even though they are quickly running out of space to raise them. Most days, they can be found planting, pulling weeds, or just enjoying a leisurely afternoon together in their yard.

◄ Jennifer is filling in a little open space with more succulents.

▲ A handful of succulent babies propagated from leaves (left) and planting succulents in a handmade wooden planter box made by Mike Pyle (right).

▼ Jennifer's front porch is bursting with not just succulents but also various green plants.

1. Have you ever counted how many plants you own?

I have no idea how many plants I have—thousands probably! I believe I have over two hundred different varieties planted throughout my gardens. I can't pass up the chance to buy the types I haven't owned yet. I have very little willpower when it comes to succulents. Some of my favorites are Echeverias, the ones that catch my eyes; some hold a special place in my heart because they are the ones that Josh loves. His favorites are Lithops, "baby toes" (Fenestraria) and "bear paws" (Cotyledon tomentosa). Over the years, I've come to appreciate every variety out there. There are many varieties with different shapes, colors, and textures to choose from!

2. There must be tons of work to do when growing a garden. Did you encounter any challenges?

The soil of the place where I live is very clay-like, which is not ideal for succulents. They prefer lighter, airier soil. Because of this, it was important to amend the soil before planting to ensure the plants' health. I did this by removing some of the clay-like soil and adding premixed cactus soil and extra pumice that can help the earth dry faster and allow the plants to take root quickly and grow with ease.

3. Your works are very creative, like the succulent shell and dreamcatchers. Where do you get such ideas?

Instead of tossing the leaves on dirt and waiting for them to grow, I would arrange them into different designs—what I call "propagation mandalas." The process of leaf propagation is slow, but it makes the waiting process more enjoyable for me. Through my fascination with succulent propagation, I came to view them as little babies. I realized that they could be planted as tiny little arrangements and live happily for months before they are removed to a larger container where they will continue to grow. I'm always trying to come up with fun ideas on how to plant succulents in unexpected ways.

If you respect and appreciate nature, you will always have a reason to smile.

◀ A handmade pot with an air plant, suspended with embroidery floss.

▲ Jennifer's bedroom sanctuary where she has created a relaxing, cozy space with numerous ornaments.

▼ With over seventy plants in her room, Jennifer spends a lot of time watering.

4. You are becoming known as one of the more successful succulent collectors. Has this fame influenced your life?

The best thing about gaining fame on Instagram is the friends I've made. I've been able to connect with many people, but I've never run my account with the intention of gaining many followers or becoming an "Instagram hit." I just wanted to share what I love, what I've learned, and connect with like-minded people. I have formed many genuine and lasting bonds with people whom I value. I share what I've learned and what I'm going through with them. I share my knowledge about caring for plants, such as tips or tricks, without reservation, and I share who I am. I want to make real connections with these people.

5. Would you share with us your philosophy about living with nature?

There is so much beauty in the world around us. If you don't take the time to see the beauty, you will miss the daily miracles. I always try to maintain a sort of "baseline of happiness." Along with appreciation comes a desire to protect. For years, Josh and I have endeavored to do our part to keep our beaches and community clean. We pick up the trash we spot on the shores and recycle some of it whenever we can. We also stay away from using plastic bags or drink boxes in Josh's school lunches. These are just little things that we've chosen to do, but it's important to remember that little things can make a big difference.

⋏ One of Jennifer's favorite cacti arrangements.

⋎ Items on shelves are purchased from small stores and artists.

➤ Jennifer fills her shelves with items she loves.

▲ Succulent pumpkins have become one of the biggest trends for fall.

▼ A tiny, living succulent wreath and a succulent shell Jennifer made and propagated.

▶ A piece from Jennifer's dreamcatcher series.

"The more time I spent appreciating the things in nature, the less I was affected by other aspects of life, especially the ones that could have brought me down."

Succulent Treat

Natural Aroma

●

"There is no better way to relax and connect with the world than by immersing ourselves in nature."

●

Ceci and Meena

Passion is like a magnet that eventually leads one to his or her dream job. Driven by the love for succulents, Ceci and Meena, the brains behind Compañía Botánica, a greenhouse located in Buenos Aires, are now pursuing their ideal careers. They cooperate with various producers and fabricate all sorts of creative plant products with the purpose of bringing greenery into people's lives.

• **Occupation:** *Owners of Compañía Botánica*
• **Location:** *Buenos Aires, Argentina*

Ceci, a trained architect, and Meena, a design graduate, met each other making pottery. They both have a background in art and design, and more importantly, they are both ardent plant lovers. Thus, they teamed up and started marketing their plant business, Compañía Botánica, focusing on creative succulent design.

In Compañía Botánica, one can find creative plant works of all kinds, ranging from succulent combs to succulent necklaces, succulent bouquets, etc. Ceci and Meena concentrate on every project, whether it takes them a few minutes or a whole week. Apart from succulents, they also promote sideline products, such as perfume, candles, and soaps, to keep a diversified business. With so many novel ideas in mind, Ceci and Meena believe that the best way to inspire other people is to connect them with nature, their inspiration and muse. "Marveling at a flower's blooming, placing our hands on the ground, enjoying the scent of aromatic herbs, and listening to the sound of the rain on the roof—the more we're close to nature, the more serenity we have. There is no better way to relax and connect with the world than by immersing ourselves in nature."

◄ Ceci and Meena's greenhouse has many of their favorite species of succulents.

▲ One of the greenhouse's most-photographed scenes.

In the beginning, Ceci and Meena just shared their lives with plants using social networks. To their surprise, they received quite a few encouraging comments, and some fans even asked them to hold workshops. They complied, and began showing more and more people how to care for cacti and succulents and how to create beautiful terrariums, kokedamas, and succulent objects on their own. In December 2017, they released a book under the same name, *Compañía Botánica*, which serves as a complete guide for cultivating plants at home. They wrote the book with the aim to help those who are struggling with their green spaces. In the book, they share their knowledge of planting, transplanting, propagation, assembling a garden, and cultivating and cooking vegetables. This book means a lot to Ceci and Meena, as they have condensed a year of work into 224 pages, through

which they hope to invite more readers to put their hands on the earth and feel the connection with nature. "Our motto is: A garden can fit in the palm of a hand," say the two.

Looking into the future, Ceci and Mena are eager to continue their work. They are anxious to broaden their horizons, travel to new places and hold their workshops, write new books, and look for inspiring ideas to create green space in houses. Apart from that, they dream of running an online shop which sells utensils, tools, garden sets, work tables, and even a whole botanical universe, so that when people click into the store, they can find support for building their green spaces and interacting with nature. They also plan to open a small greenhouse to the public where they will serve dishes and drinks made from ingredients from their orchard.

◀ Plants of different shapes and textures hang on the wall.

▲ Ceci and Meena most enjoy design and custom work because of the creative energy involved.

▼ Ceci and Meena are in the process of selecting succulent cuttings to create a bridal bouquet.

▲ The basic materials to assemble a succulent crown including succulent cuttings, substrate, wire, moss, and tools.

▼ Shaping the crown by wrapping moss, substrate and wire.

▲ Drilling holes in the moss with a stick, where succulents will be inserted.

▼ The final design depends on imagination and creativity.

....

1. Why do you choose succulents?

Succulents stand out with their beautiful forms, colors, and textures; they are easy to grow and require little maintenance and water. Thus, they are ideal for urban cultivation in general. We have been collecting them for years. One day, we came across a pottery workshop, and we began thinking of making pots on our own. It was in that moment when we started working on both plants and designs.

2. Your works are creative and functional. How do you come up with your ideas?

For many years, human beings have been using natural elements—branches, wildflowers, and fruit—to celebrate and decorate on special days. We like to recreate these traditional arrangements by using succulents, not only because they bear lovely shapes and colors, but also because they have long lifespans. Many of our works are based on traditional ideas and old subjects. For example, foliage crowns are usually discarded after a period of time. To make a change, we use slices of succulent and tie them with thread, so that they can last for weeks; what's more, if we untie these succulents, we can replant them. The same technique can be adopted for succulent necklaces, bridal bouquets, and brooches—we call them "alive accessories." They are like an event reminder that keeps a memory alive.

3. What role does social media play in your plant business?

In the past four years, many things have changed on the social platforms with the birth of new networks and new ways of communication. We consider social networks to be an important tool, not only because of the content they convey, but also the impact they bring. We are always attentive to what is happening around us, and we try to use that information for our benefit. When we founded our brand online, we planned to use it to upload photos only because back then there weren't too many options for filters or apps. But over the years, video-sharing has become popular, so now we generate video clips and share them on Instagram using

> **"**
>
> *We believe that the best way to inspire other people is to transmit the connection with nature in a lively way.*
>
> **"**

◄ The motto of Compañía Botánica is, "A garden can fit in the palm of a hand."

▲ ▼ The sculptural forms of the plants and the mixture between vintage and modern inspire Ceci and Meena to create botanical displays.

time lapse, boomerang, rewind and other tools that the app provides. In fact, online sharing has brought us success, and we can generate connections with our audience and produce aesthetic and creative content whenever and wherever we like. For us, the live options on Instagram and Facebook are opportunities, and we're experimenting with live workshops where we offer greenhouse classes for larger audiences.

4. Apart from the succulents, Compañía Botánica also sells perfume, candles, and aromatherapy supplies. What is so special about these sideline products?

We find it interesting to create products that are related to the philosophy of Compañía Botánica. We extract essential oils from aromatic herbs and spices. To seek more inspiration, we imagine ourselves having a picnic on the riverbank on a spring afternoon, fresh lemonades in hands, fresh air on our faces. We named it "botanic alchemy" because we like to picture ourselves as modern alchemists who work with aromas and essences. The packaging aims to display that idea, and for several products' packaging, we use some laboratory elements. One of our perfumes, "Botanical Inspiration," is popular among both men and women for its fresh smell. It contains essential oils of nardo, bergamot, ginger, and a secret note. The name comes from one of our favorite hashtags, and it includes the essence that we like to convey. Along with this aroma, we create a line of soaps, candles, and bath salts.

5. What's your favorite thing about life in Buenos Aires?

Life in Buenos Aires is super inspiring because of the large number of museums, exhibitions, cultural events, and design work! Going out to eat or have a drink, meeting friends, and having exciting encounters are things that happen all the time. But what we love most is to see the trees changing through the seasons. In spring, the streets and avenues are colored with blue jacarandas, making it a dreamlike city.

⋀ A selection of succulents are ready for a new terrarium.
⋁ Working tools including shovels, shears, and pots.
➤ A corner of Compañía Botánica.

▲ Succulent terrariums in glass houses.
▼ Succulent arrangements in vintage pots.
➤ A beautiful succulent wreath.

"To live among nature is to connect with its rhythms and cycles, to observe and respect the times that nature imposes, and eventually to perceive and enjoy it with all our senses!"

Vitally Vines
An Indoor Garden

•

*"I feel full of life. Evolution makes me
excited; it keeps me alive."*

•

Fem Güçlütürk

Fem Güçlütürk used to live in an apartment in Istanbul. Crammed with
distinctive objects that she has collected during her journeys around the
world, the apartment was a world of plants and ceramics. She focuses
on learning the plants' language, living with them, and integrating her
life's philosophy with them. Recently, Fem moved to Muğla to continue
purchasing her ideal life with plants.

••

• **Occupation:** *Urban plant enthusiast*
• **Location:** *Muğla, Turkey*

Fem Güçlütürk's enthusiasm for plants started years ago when she moved to a terrace house in 1996, where the previous tenant left several potted plants. As Fem moved in, her passion for plants gradually grew. Hundreds of jars of tropical plants were scattered through every corner of her house in Istanbul, including ferns, cacti, and succulents. Walking into this place was like roaming in an enchanting botanical garden where greens blended with modern architecture. The plants brought not only clean air to the space, but also adorned everything with liveliness. But keeping so many pots indoors is not easy.

Once, a severe earthquake struck the area where she lived. After the quake, her neighbors sued her for the heavy load on the terrace that she had caused, with all her plants and the water needed to feed them. When the judge came, he checked around, but then laughed and left without penalizing her.

Fem enjoys all the stages of plant growth, from its birth to flourishing. Every one of her collections comes with a tiny "passport" with a description of the plant and instructions for care. She once ran a plant shop called "Labofem" in Istanbul, which was in business for over four years, where she sold plants in unique vessels and compositions. Labofem was also a greenhouse where she learned how to listen to the plants and share their stories with people around the world. But she closed this lush operation for a personal reason in 2017 and decided to move to Muğla. "If I am not in the shop myself, there is no fun anymore. The reason for Labofem's existence is not just to sell pots of plants but to translate the plants' language to humans, so that they can survive! I read, study, and learn new stuff about plants every day. I believe there will be new life and new beginnings ahead," Fem explains. Though the physical shop is closed, Fem says that Labofem will evolve as a channel on YouTube, on which she will share people's lives in Muğla.

◄ ▲ ▼ Fem's balcony of her Istanbul house used to be a little garden with succulents and cacti widely distributed in every corner.

For Fem, the way she lives is the way she views the world. Having dabbled in different fields, such as tourism, entertainment, operations, management, and brand consultancy, she has made various choices in life and gone through many changes. As such, she likes to reconfigure her surroundings often, by adjusting her plants' positions and rearranging the furniture. "I like to renew my living conditions, meet new people, and collect new stories. I like to change professions and even the husbands I marry!" she jokes. "I have only one life, and I want to color it. Plants are my friends; we have a good time," adds Fem.

Fem loves traveling and has been to many countries, including Sri Lanka, Guatemala, Jamaica, Mozambique, Iceland, and Israel. All these places have created different stories for Fem. At this moment, her favorite place is the subtropical Muğla province in southern Turkey. Olive and daphne trees surround the area, the weather is warm, the population is small but happy, and most importantly, nature stays undisturbed. "No car toots, no traffic jams. Just earth, wind, and fire!" Fem believes that it is far better than living in the city. Throughout the year, each season brings different joys and surprises. "After tasting that delicious fruit, worshiping the ground, smelling the fresh air, loving the centipedes, caring for the worms, hearing the birds singing above my head, witnessing how my plants connect with Mother Nature, and thriving again with the help of natural spring water, I realized that the time had come—it was time to wake up to a magical planet called Earth in this magical village."

◄ Hundreds of plants have taken up Fem's Istanbul home space.
▲ A big window with plenty of sunlight provides plants with nutrients.
▼ Wooden chairs showcase certain specimens.

1. You used to work for a PR company. Why did you turn to the plant field?

In that job, I started to feel meaningless and disturbed in my work—trying to convince or press people on the products and services that personally I don't consume or need at all! And my relationship with potted plants was an issue for years. In those years, I was busy working and traveling the world, especially with my enduro motorbike, and visiting botanic parks on my way. Thus, I didn't have much time to put my fingers into the soil. All my knowledge came from books and stayed organized in Excel files. I had a huge list of plants with Latin names, nicknames, pH needs, sun needs, watering needs, etc. One day, I was staying in the home of a Copenhagen artist who has a home with tiny triangle windows and beautiful porcelain pots with seeds on her windowsills. I thought, why not bring the containers to Turkey, where we have more sun, more space, and a subtropical climate. And then I said to myself, "Let's give it a try!"

2. There were more than a thousand pots of plants in your place. Why did you raise so many plants at home?

If you start to collect plants you can't stop! You want to meet other plant friends. Each of them are unique and adorable. I hunted local no-name ceramic students and artists, and convinced them to work for Labofem only. They were as excited as I was. With an aesthetic outlook and botanical practice, plants and their ceramic masterpieces look and live great together!

3. There must be a lot of memories from running Labofem those four years. Would you share some?

Yes—we had a lot of visitors from all over the world, like from Sweden, Holland, Japan, Germany, Brazil, Pakistan, France, and the Ukraine. The shop was a hidden paradise, but our foreign visitors found it anyway. Even our neighbors called us many times to get directions because they couldn't find the building! I had a couple of customers who had sent plants with funny messages to each other, and they came to

> *There are many ways that living species communicate. To be able to communicate with them, we have to learn how to be silent and to listen.*

◄ Cacti collection outside Labofem.

▲ ▼ Labofem was like a tropical botanical garden where visitors could explore for hours.

revisit when they got married, got pregnant, and had a baby. Plant addicts from all over the world shared their stories in my peaceful paradise—what a fantastic thing! Now they have become good friends of mine and will visit me in my new place. The shop was not like a shop; it was a meeting place for plant lovers. I remember one day I opened the shop in the morning and saw a cat staring at me from among the plants, and then she left the room with careful, graceful movements. She didn't break or eat or destroy a single plant.

4. You once said, "It is fulfilling to observe the life cycle of plants and learn their language." In your opinion, what is the plants' language?

There are many ways that living species communicate. To be able to communicate with them, we have to learn how to be silent and to listen. If you look deeper into a plant, you'll learn a lot from its color, smell, shape, and texture. Listening is not literally listening. What I mean by listening to plants is to look closer, to observe, to smell, and to touch.

5. Where do you see yourself going in the future?

Who knows! But it seems Muğla will be my place—until I find the next. People think that it's not good to change lifestyles so frequently. I ask them: Why? If you are done with it, please move on. You don't have to negotiate with your current situation to be happy. We shouldn't be afraid of change because there is nothing permanent except change. So why not change your lifestyle if you don't like it? What we call life is constantly changing—it's not something that we can foresee! Things can happen at any time. That's why I can't tell where I will end up, whether in an hour or in the distant future. The only philosophy I have is to be grateful when I wake up healthy every morning, with food and shelter, and friends with whom I can share my life. That's all. We are lucky to be in the three percent of the world's population who can have food just by ordering it from the menu of a restaurant. That is more than enough to be grateful for, isn't it?

▲ ▼ Transplanting a succulent.
➤ Greenery in harmony with a vintage wooden desk in Labofem.

▲ ▼ ➤ Fem's collections of cacti and succulents in different shapes and species are presented in all kinds of ceramics.

"I never realized in detail where the sun comes up and where it goes down, but now I know. In the past, I was not a fan of insects. Now I'm talking to them."

Index

Lush Leaf

Ivan Martinez and Christan Summers · Brooklyn, New York, USA

Photography: Stephen Yang for FAD Market (p052), Tula Plants and Design

www.tula.house

P052-063

Wona Bae and Charlie Lawler · Melbourne, Australia

www.looseleafstore.com.au

P064-075

Josh Rosen · Santa Monica, California, USA

www.airplantman.com

P076-089

Floral

Anna Potter · Sheffield, UK
Photography: India Hobson
www.swallowsanddamsons.com
P092-103

Claire Basler · Château de Beauvoir, Échassières, France
www.clairebasler.com
P104-117

Olga Prinku · Yarm, UK
www.prinku.com
P118-131

Manuela Sosa Gianoni · Barcelona, Spain

Photography: Lara Lopez (p132-137), Marta Sanchez Umami (p138-143)

www.gangandthewool.com

P132-143

Hanna Wendelbo · Gothenburg, Sweden

www.hannawendelbo.com

P144-155

Fiona Pickles · West Yorkshire, UK

Photography: Nicola Dixon (p156, 158, 169), Melia Melia photography (p159-161, 162 photo below, 163-167), Naomi Kenton (p168 photo above), Holly Rattray (p168 photo below), Tessa Bunney (p162 photo above)

www.firenzafloraldesign.co.uk

P156-169

Miniature

Maja, Cille and Gro · Copenhagen, Denmark

Photography: Kaktus København

www.kaktuskbh.dk

P172-183

Antonio Jotta and Carol Nóbrega · São Paulo, Brazil

Photography: Angelo Dal Bó, Karen Suehiro

www.atelierbotanico.com

P184-197

Noam Levy · Paris, France

www.greenfactory.fr

P198-211

Jennifer Tao • Camarillo, California, USA

Photography: Rebecca Stevens (p212, 214)

www.instagram.com/jenssuccs/
www.botanicalbright.com

P212-223

Ceci and Meena • Buenos Aires, Argentina

Photography: Rosario Lanusse (p224-231), Compañía Botánica (p232-237)

www.ciabotanica.com.ar

P224-237

Fem Güçlütürk • Muğla, Turkey

www.labofem.com

P238-249

Acknowledgements

We would like to express our gratitude to all of the artists and designers, studios and companies for their generous contribution of images, ideas, and concepts. We are also very grateful to many other people whose names do not appear in the credits but who made specific contributions and provided support. Without them, the successful completion of this book would not be possible. Special thanks to all of the contributors for sharing their innovation and creativity with all of our readers around the world. Our editorial team includes editors Zhang Zhonghui, Jessie Tan, Swing Xian and book designer Chow Pakwah, to whom we are truly grateful.